A Matter of Life and Death in Texas

Chuck Cox

Copyright © 2017 Chuck Cox
All rights reserved.

ISBN: 0692846832
ISBN 13: 9780692846834
Library of Congress Control Number: 2017902765
Surfing Steve Publishing, Dallas, TX

DEDICATION

For David McNabb and Brian Williams. Rest in peace, my friends.

PROLOGUE

Officers Borger and Overton were on their way to eat their favorite chicken fried steak dinner at Taylor's Café when they received a call on the radio there had been an accident on Farm-to-Market Road 38.

They immediately raced over with the lights on and the siren blaring from their police cruiser. They arrived at the scene a couple of minutes before the ambulance. As the Trinity Springs Police Department officers pulled up, they saw a battered car resting on an embankment upside down.

Outside of the faint sound of the hazard lights blinking on the white Ford Futura, there was an eerie silence as they made their way to the wreckage. Officer Borger recognized the vehicle right away, causing a sickening feeling in the pit of his stomach.

Officer Overton knelt down to look inside the car. He saw a teenage girl bleeding badly who did not appear to be breathing. He reached in and grabbed her right wrist.

No pulse.

1

GRAHAM CHANDLER

Graham Chandler peeked at the digital clock on the dusty dashboard of his burnt orange 1972 Volkswagen Beetle. After another grueling Texas summer, his car was somehow even more faded than it was the last time it was at Trinity Springs High School.

7:49 a.m.

Graham's tires squealed as he narrowly missed hitting the curb underneath the big, purple sign that read in bold letters: "Trinity Springs High School. Home of the Sidewinders."

The "s" at the end of "Sidewinders" was a rattlesnake shaped like the letter. Graham always thought that was pretty bad ass.

Somehow he was actually early.

Even Graham was astonished considering "Tardy" had become his unofficial nickname among the school's teachers during his junior year. So much so that some of the faculty members solely referred to him by that moniker.

Graham's car also had an unofficial nickname. Several of his friends had taken to calling his ride "The Nazi Mobile," which made Graham cringe every single time they did.

But his hand-me-down ride from his cousin Vivian, from Alexandria, Louisiana, had turned out to be a pretty damn good mode of transportation. Especially considering it cost him a whopping $700 with the family discount.

His car was also only seven bucks to fill up, which was just about perfect for Graham's miniscule budget.

The Beetle had a bit of an odd smell permeating from somewhere under the backseat, faded shoe polish on the exterior paint from his friends lovingly decorating it and a stereo that was probably worth slightly more than the car itself.

And, sure, Graham had to rapidly pump the brakes just to get the damn things to work, which would occasionally make for a moment of panic at a stop sign or red light. But the car was all his — signed, sealed and delivered.

Plus, "The Slug Bug," the nickname Graham very much preferred for his car, had allowed him to spend precious time with his girlfriend Katy Christoval, who never owned a car in her life.

Once he finally got a driver's license and then the car, it also meant he no longer had to climb aboard the bus to get to and from school. That was also a pretty enormous selling point.

Graham would have driven just about anything with four wheels — and, of course, a good stereo — to make that a reality. Although, not coincidentally, vehicular independence was also the gateway drug to his perpetual tardiness.

After their families met in East Texas to bring the car to Graham, he washed it in his driveway every few days for the first few weeks it was his — even though the car pretty much looked the same clean or dirty.

Graham often imagined what the car must have looked like when it was shiny and new, rolling off the assembly line with glistening burnt orange paint.

There was also the car's ridiculously wimpy sounding horn that had to eventually work its way into Graham's heart. The thing sounded like it could barely convince a squirrel running across the road to get out of the way.

As he pulled into one of the front parking spaces reserved for members of the senior class, Graham sat quietly in the driver's seat and stared at the clock, watching it change over from 7:52 to 7:53 a.m. He could hear his fellow seniors parking their cars in close proximity with their stereos blaring.

With the exception of the faculty parking lot, the senior parking spots were the closest ones to the high school. Graham was looking forward to the upgrade in proximity after parking way the hell out in B.F.E. his junior year.

Plus, parking closer was bound to give Graham at least a sporting chance of being on time for school. He figured his odds would go up to at least 55/45.

"Fucking first day of school," he muttered, as he ran both of his palms across his hairless baby face. His brown hair, as always, was cut short and free of any styling products.

Graham typically got his hair cut once a month at the old barbershop downtown. He loved that the place still had a red, white and blue barber's pole that spun by the front door.

If his hair got the least bit shaggy, Graham felt compelled to immediately get it trimmed. He liked the fact he didn't have to bother making it look good when he rolled out of bed or after basketball practice.

Graham reached into his pocket and pulled out his black wallet that still had a faint hint of new smell. He opened the wallet and removed his favorite photo of Katy, the one he had taken of her outside the school's theater one February afternoon after she had finished a one-act play dress rehearsal.

Katy had her blonde hair pulled back into a ponytail and was still wearing the costume for her role as Eliza Doolittle in *Pygmalion*.

It seemed like a lifetime ago Graham had taken that picture, which was a little bent at the corners from being tucked into his wallet for the last six months.

Small tears began to stream down Graham's cheeks as the clock hit 7:54 a.m. He closed his eyes, quickly wiped the tears away and carefully placed Katy's photo back into his wallet. She had bought the wallet for him the previous Christmas.

Katy wrapped the wallet in white wrapping paper adorned with basketballs and basketball hoops with orange ribbon and a matching bow. She wrote on the tag: "Merry Christmas, sweetie. I love you always — KC." He still had that tag in the top drawer of his dresser along with movie and game ticket stubs he had collected over the years.

Even though Graham knew Katy was really gone, it still felt like some endless nightmare from which he could never seem to awaken.

All summer he kept thinking Katy would call him or show up at his house any minute wearing his black and purple letter jacket, looking and smelling like an absolute living, breathing dream. Even at her worst, Katy was so amazingly beautiful. And she seemingly never stopped smiling.

"Hey, gorgeous," she would say almost every time she saw Graham, never once failing to make him smile. "Look who's talking," he'd reply to her before they would kiss and say they loved one another.

Graham closed his eyes, remembering how Katy's kisses tasted and the way her voice sounded. She typically had an enthusiastic tone that would quickly put anybody talking to her in a good mood.

Of course, there was also her ever-present Texas drawl that she had even way back in junior high when they first met. Katy could add two or three syllables to pretty much any word with her drawn-out pronunciations, which was especially endearing to Graham.

"Look who's talking," he muttered under his breath.

Graham quickly gathered himself and looked at his blue eyes in the rearview mirror to make sure they weren't bloodshot. It was time to put on a brave face. He had come to learn in the last three months that was absolutely essential to maintaining any sense of his sanity.

The more he looked like he had his shit completely together, the less chance he'd have to engage in a long conversation about what happened to Katy for the umpteenth time. Talking about the accident never got easier.

Graham promised himself he would keep his upper lip stiff on the first day of school. He also wondered how hard it might be to really pull off that trick — especially since it was his senior year.

He figured he was sure to hear, "Oh, Graham, I'm so sorry about Katy," several times over the course of the first day. He knew he would also get a healthy dose of those familiar sympathetic looks.

Graham lost count of how many times he had seen those sad looks over the summer, but he was determined to not let his emotions get the best of him this day. He knew things were bound to get better if he could just get through day one. But it was hard. The painful memories vividly replayed in his mind like a movie.

Katy died in a car wreck right after their junior year ended — May 24, 1986, to be exact. It was the evening after the Class of 1986 seniors walked the stage, got their diplomas and moved the tassels to the other side of their caps.

It was also a rare Saturday night Graham wasn't with Katy. He had hung out with his dad, Miles, all day before he got the phone call from Katy's mom around 7:30 p.m. Graham's Dad left to go home a couple of hours earlier.

It took Graham nearly 15 minutes to stop shaking after he heard the tragic news. He was on his bed sobbing until his mom, Donna, got home from shopping with one of her friends. They hugged and cried together for more than an hour before they finally went to Katy's house to be with her parents.

Graham and Katy were together until 11:30 p.m. the night before the accident. They went to the graduation ceremony to see some of their friends in the senior class get their diplomas.

They then went for ice cream, drove around town and talked, which was one of their absolute favorite things to do together. Those were the kind of evenings when Graham truly loved that his "Slug Bug" had a sun roof. Graham imagined his car was a brand new Corvette with the breeze blowing into their hair as they drove for miles and miles.

Graham didn't sleep the night Katy died. Or for the next two nights. He was overwhelmed with intense disbelief and sorrow, but exhaustion eventually won out early Tuesday morning.

The best he could remember, the day Katy died was one of only five or six Saturdays they hadn't seen each other in at least a year. Most of the Saturdays they weren't together were because Miles was visiting from Dallas. Graham's parents got divorced not long after he met Katy.

When Miles was in town, Katy would occasionally tag along to lunch or dinner, but she wanted Graham to have plenty of quality time alone with him. Her parents were still married, which was something she never took for granted. Like most people who knew them, Katy had always believed Donna and Miles seemed like a perfect couple.

It took Graham a couple of weeks after the accident to mildly feel like himself again and to begin the long process of picking up the pieces. But not one single day went by he didn't think about Katy. Her memory was everywhere — at home, at the mall, at church … and now at school.

All of the Trinity Springs High School students, faculty and staff seemingly showed up for Katy's funeral, which was the Friday after she died. There were people standing outside of the jam-packed pews and up against the wall in the church.

Graham remembered how warm it was in the church because of all of the people. He also remembered he had almost sweated through his new black suit minutes after arriving for the funeral. Seeing all of the love everybody had for Katy was really the only good thing he could recall about that awful day.

Graham pushed the thought aside as he finally opened his car door. As one of his white Kaepa tennis shoes with the blue arrows snapped onto the sides hit the pavement, Kyle Utley, Graham's best friend since the second grade, slapped his hand on the back of the Beetle with authority and bellowed loudly, "The Nazi Mobile!"

Kyle lovingly hugged the back side of the car, drawing glances from a couple of fellow seniors who were already making their way to school. Once they realized it was Kyle, they immediately ignored their class clown and went back to what they were doing.

This time, the uncomfortable nickname for his car actually made Graham smile — only because it made everything seem more normal. Plus, Kyle was really a sight for sore eyes after he had been on vacation with his family in Denver the previous week.

The Utleys didn't get back from Colorado until late Sunday evening. Graham hadn't had a chance to talk to Kyle before they finally embarked on their senior year — a day that had dreamed of and discussed, ad nauseam, for the previous three school years.

"How were the Rocky Mountains? Did you meet any hot Colorado chicks?"

"You bet your ass I did," Kyle answered, grinning widely. "Two or three really hot ones, as a matter of fact. You know the ladies are drawn to me like white on rice, Chandler."

"Bullshit!"

The two best friends laughed and shook hands while Graham's car was still making odd noises, even though the engine had been killed for several seconds.

After Graham made sure the car finally fell silent, they walked up to the front doors of the school, passing the big marquee sign that read: "WELCOME, SENIORS. CLASS OF 1987." The individual letters and numbers on the marquee were all black, except for the 9, which was blue.

Graham and Kyle looked at the sign and shared that same surreal and exciting feeling that the finish line was finally in sight. After three long years, it had finally come down to nine more months until their ultimate freedom from high school.

Almost to the school's main entrance, Graham noticed a few of his classmates looking at him and whispering to one another. Kyle also noticed. He quickly tried to distract his best friend with conversation about one of their favorite subjects — basketball.

"Can you believe we're seniors, dude? We're winning state this year, man. I just fucking know we are. With Henderson and Wylie back, plus you and me, nobody's beating us, right? Not even Prescott. Right, Graham?"

Graham made eye contact with Kyle and slowly nodded in approval without uttering a word. He really was looking forward to basketball season more than ever. For starters, Kyle was absolutely right — the team was going to be incredibly good, maybe even the best in school history.

Graham also longed to get back into his familiar basketball routine, even though part of that daily grind involved running endless amounts of laps for Coach Elgin during practice. Graham was more than ready for that kind of distraction from constantly thinking about Katy.

Although Graham and the majority of his teammates were not exactly the biggest fans in the world of Coach Elgin, they all knew the guy was extremely good at his job — even if he was a hard ass of the highest order.

"Get your asses in gear!" he would scream at least three times each practice, in between making Graham and his teammates run like race horses over and over in that sweaty-ass gym.

His whistle echoed loudly in the cavernous space each time they finished a complete trip up and down the court. They couldn't stop running until he quickly blew the whistle twice. Some days it seemed like they ran for a good 15 minutes without a breather.

Graham also swore Coach Elgin cranked up the heat at least 10 degrees before practice every day because that gym was normally as cold as a witch's tit in a brass bra. Hell, you'd get chill bumps within five seconds of walking into that place any other time of the day the Sidewinders weren't practicing. Graham once walked into the gym and saw his breath.

Graham even heard that damn whistle blowing in his sleep. But he knew Coach Elgin was more than capable of leading them to Austin in March for the state basketball tournament and guiding the Sidewinders to that coveted state championship. That was really all that mattered.

They all knew deep down their head coach being a hard ass was part of what helped make them such a good team. And the guy damn sure knew his X's and O's like the back of his hand.

Graham remembered scanning the crowd at Katy's funeral and seeing his ball-busting coach wipe the tears from his red eyes and the sweat off his brow with a handkerchief while standing up against a wall.

Graham was in the second row, squeezed in between his parents and Katy's parents in a pew. He made eye contact with Coach Elgin for a few seconds, and Graham could see the deepest sympathy for him in his eyes.

That particular moment really stood out in Graham's mind since it was pretty much the only time he'd ever seen a look like that from him. In fact, it was one of the most comforting things Graham remembered from the day they laid the love of his life to rest.

On cue, Kermit Henderson and Vernon Wylie walked in the hall as Graham and Kyle were walking into the welcoming blast of air conditioning right in their path.

"Look at this shit here, Kermit. We're in the presence of the sorriest damn backcourt in District 22-3A. That one wouldn't know an assist if it bit him on the ass," Vernon said, motioning to Kyle.

"Shit, I helped make you the district MVP last season, if I remember correctly," Kyle rapidly snapped back to Vernon. The teammates then loudly exchanged high-fives and hugs, causing a minor traffic jam in the busy foyer.

"How are you, Chandler?" Kermit asked.

"I'm good, bro. I'm good."

"Utley? How was the Mile High State?"

"Fuck you," Kyle replied, making sure no teachers happened to be walking nearby to hear his colorful choice of language.

"Such hostility and anger on the very first day of school," Kermit said, condescendingly. "Have you boys been practicing hard this summer? Shooting some free throws? We're going to the Drum this year, damn it. And you two are going to help us get there and win that state title. I want my fucking trophy AND my fucking ring!"

"Damn right," Graham answered enthusiastically.

"All right, fellas," Vernon said. "We'll catch y'all later."

"Later," Graham and Kyle said in unison.

Kermit and Vernon walked away together as the warning bell rang loudly, sending a mild wave of panic throughout the hallways. Before they headed off for class, Kyle placed his hand on Graham's right shoulder.

"It's going to be all good, bro. Any time you need us, we're here. You know that, right? We are your family. We're your teammates. You tell us if you need anything."

"I will," Graham said with a smile finally coming back to his face. "Thanks, Kyle."

The two of them said their goodbyes and headed in opposite directions to their first class of the new school year. Being seniors already made the first day have a significantly different vibe than previous years, but the fact it was also the first day of school without Katy compounded the feeling for Graham.

After consulting his schedule card, Graham confirmed he would be in English IV with Mrs. Hitchcock for first period, Room 108.

He had never met Mrs. Hitchcock, but he heard stories about her from seniors on the basketball team over the previous couple of years. They said some of the students called her "Vertigo" because her excessive homework assignments made their heads spin. Plus, there was the whole Alfred Hitchcock movie reference thing.

Graham was well aware he was in for some serious brutality once he was a senior in her class. She was the only teacher at the school who taught English IV, aka Senior English.

He had hoped Katy would be in the same class with him so they could help each other out. He also hoped English IV wouldn't be first damn period, since that's when Graham was most likely to be late.

Katy was always good at English. It wasn't Graham's worst subject, but it damn sure wasn't his best subject, either. He was not at all ready for another ball-busting authority figure in his life.

"One is plenty," he said to himself as he quickly made his way down the hall and past Katy's locker from the previous year. He glanced at the purple locker as he hurried to class. Graham and Katy had several conversations in front of that locker, the subjects of which were usually what they were doing that weekend, Trinity Springs basketball or trying to find Kyle a girlfriend.

"Kyle needs to get himself a woman, Graham," Katy would say. "There has got to be somebody out there for him, right? Maybe we need to look at girls at other high schools."

As Graham walked through the door of Room 108, the small talk and general buzz in the classroom fell awkwardly silent. He looked for a seat and gave a slight nod to a few of his classmates while trying to ignore the silence but, as usual, it was deafening.

He sat down in an empty chair in the middle of the classroom, which caused a loud squeak that put a merciful end to the silence.

After settling in and giving a cursory look around the room, he took a new folder out of his new notebook. Graham started to make the pristine folder his own.

He wrote: English IV. First Period. Room 108. Hitchcock.

Graham also drew out big block letters to spell "V-E-R-T-I-G-O" in the middle of the folder. He also did his best to draw the Golden Gate Bridge, although it looked like it could have been pretty much any bridge in the world other than the Golden Gate.

Everyone eventually started their conversations back up, much to the delight of Graham, who was solely concentrating on his doodling as the final loud seconds of the last bell rang.

All of the conversation came to a screeching halt again when Elsa Hitchcock finally made her way into the classroom with a steaming cup of coffee in her right hand and a pile of books and papers in her left hand. She walked with great purpose and immediately seemed like she was clearly no fan of bullshit.

Mrs. Hitchcock was one of those spitfire types. She was an attractive blonde in her early thirties. She stood about five-foot-nothing and weighed maybe 95 pounds soaking wet, but there was attitude in pretty much every ounce of her being.

More like Psycho, Graham thought, causing him to smirk a little bit as he put aside his makeshift art work.

Graham looked around the classroom once again. He recognized almost everybody since he had gone to school with almost all of his classmates since kindergarten.

Trinity Springs Elementary, Trinity Springs Junior High and Trinity Springs High School all stood right beside one another — bam, bam, bam. Anonymity was never a menu option in this neck of the woods.

To his surprise, Graham suddenly noticed a dude he had never seen sitting three seats over in the row in front of him. He was intrigued at the thought of a new student starting school his senior year. Graham immediately felt somewhat bad for the new guy.

He could not imagine going to high school somewhere for three years, moving the last year and having to start all over making friends and learning an entirely different environment.

Although Graham was fully aware of how great Trinity Springs High School was, this kid had to walk into a new situation blindly. For all he knew, this could be an absolutely horrible place to go to school.

Man, how bad does that suck to graduate from a school you only went to for only one damn year? I'm sure he'll know about me and Katy before the day is over. Hell, he'll probably know before this class is over.

That's the way things are in a small town. Everybody knows everybody else's business, which is only compounded by being in the high school environment.

Pretty much any time anything out of the norm happened, it was the buzz around school for days, sometimes weeks. The bigger the story, the bigger and longer the fuss made. That shit could sometimes drag out for a whole six weeks.

Graham continued to look over the new guy as Mrs. Hitchcock said "Hello, class," and gathered herself. She finally started to call roll as everybody in class was finally quiet and paying attention to her.

The new guy didn't look like he was from anywhere near Trinity Springs. In fact, he kind of had that ahead-of-the-curve look, sort of like Kevin Bacon's character, Ren McCormack, in *Footloose*. Cool clothes, cool haircut … the works.

Graham and Katy saw that movie together on their first real date at the mall, which was a generous term considering the Trinity Springs Mall consisted of about two dozen crappy stores and only a slightly better two-screen movie theater.

If anybody in town wanted to go to a real mall or have more than two movie options, they had to make the 90-minute drive to either Austin or San Antonio.

Still, it was the only movie theater in town. And it was the perfect place for Graham and Katy to go on dates and share popcorn while they watched movies from the back row — just like they were adults.

Graham remembered how Katy would smile at him while she was sprinkling Raisinettes into the bucket of buttered popcorn practically every time they were there.

He recalled her singing along with some of the songs in *Footloose* under her breath — especially the title track and "Holding Out for a Hero" — while she chomped on her popcorn. She would let out a little gasp of excitement when a bite included a piece of candy.

This new guy had his sandy blond hair spiked straight up, a blue and white vertical striped shirt, acid washed jeans and cool black boots. Once Graham got a look at his face, he thought the guy even vaguely resembled Kevin Bacon.

Man, this dude is going to be bored out of his fucking mind in this town.

Graham made sure to catch his name when Mrs. Hitchcock got to him during roll call. She had made her way quickly through the first half of the alphabet before calling out Erin Mansfield.

Graham glanced over at Erin, who was sitting one row behind him on his right, and gave her a smile. She replied, "Here," while maintaining eye contact with Graham, giving him the best smile back she could muster.

Graham could tell right away from the look in her eyes Erin had been thinking about Katy, which he fully expected would be the case.

From the beginning, Erin and Katy hit it off like Raisinettes and buttered popcorn. It was almost like they were lifelong friends the minute they met in junior high. The two of them quickly became inseparable.

If Katy wasn't with Graham, she was most likely with Erin. Like Graham, Katy was an only child, so she very much considered Erin a sister.

In fact, it shattered Erin every bit as much as it did Graham when Katy died. And with the possible exception of Kyle, nobody had been more of a shoulder to cry on for Graham than Erin — and vice versa.

They had spent so much time together over the summer that Graham also started to feel like Erin was the sister he never had. Most times they commiserated, looked at pictures of Katy, swapped stories about her and cried. Erin was essential to Graham being able to pick up the pieces — and vice versa.

"She loved you so much," Erin had told Graham so many times after Katy died. "You were her world, Graham."

Mrs. Hitchcock continued calling roll.

"Tyler Nixon."

That was the one — the only unfamiliar name of the bunch. And the new guy replied with a quick, confident and extremely cool, "Yo."

Just so he wouldn't forget it, Graham pulled out his notebook and jotted down Tyler's name right underneath his V-E-R-T-I-G-O lettering and makeshift Golden Gate Bridge. As he did, Mrs. Hitchcock introduced Tyler to the class, which only consisted of a total of about 20 students.

"Say hello to Tyler Nixon, class. Today is his first day at Trinity Springs. Let's all make him feel welcome and a part of this senior class — just like he's been here all along with us."

The class dutifully said "Hello, Tyler," in something that did not even mildly resemble unison.

Graham figured he would introduce himself to the new kid after class to make him feel at home. He also wanted to ask him if he played basketball and where he moved from. Graham was surprised Hitch had not mentioned his previous school when she introduced Tyler.

Graham figured Tyler was probably from some bustling metropolis that was the anti-Trinity Springs — a place that had a theater with more than two screens and a real mall. He damn sure wouldn't be able to put together his first day of school ensemble with the help of either of the two clothing stores in Trinity Springs.

The first day of school usually meant no homework, but not in Hitch's class. Near the end of the period, she assigned her new group of seniors to read the first two chapters of *Wuthering Heights* by the next day.

She doled out copies of the book from a big box that had been hidden underneath her desk and was hastily labeled "WH" in black lettering by a magic marker.

Several students looked at her in disbelief for assigning homework on the first damn day of school, but that only made Mrs. Hitchcock feel kind of warm and fuzzy inside.

Reading the first two chapters of any love story was about the last thing Graham wanted to do. Especially a love story written long before he was born that promised to be about as exciting as a *Murder, She Wrote* marathon.

But as the bell to signal the end of first period finally rang, he packed up the same backpack he'd had for the last three years, slipped his slightly worn-out copy of *Wuthering Heights* inside and got up from his squeaky chair.

He was about to flag down Tyler, who darted out of his seat, when Erin cut off his path and met him with a hug.

"Are you okay, sweetie?" she said, studying Graham's face to see if she could determine his answer before she heard it. "I know you're missing Katy lots today."

"I'm good," Graham said. Strangely, the first real mention of the subject of Katy was much less upsetting than he thought it would be — probably because it was coming from Erin. He figured she would likely be the first one to bring up Katy's name, so he was kind of prepared for it.

"I know the first day of school is hard," she said as she started to tear up. "It's so weird not having her here today. She should be sitting in this class, right here with us. I miss her so damn much, Graham."

"I do, too. It's like I expect to see her in the halls or standing at her locker, you know? I can almost hear her laughing or her voice saying my name."

Erin nodded as a couple more tears fell from her big blue eyes.

Graham wiped away her tears, gave her another hug and a kiss on the cheek and told her, "Be strong."

"You know Katy wouldn't want us to be all sad and to mope around, right?" Graham said, looking Erin directly in the eyes. She nodded in agreement.

Graham said goodbye and scurried out of Vertigo's classroom to try to still catch Tyler, but the new guy was already way too far down the hallway.

Plus, Graham still had to get to his next class, on the other side of the building, on time. He was bound and determined not to be late for any classes on the first day of school.

Graham could faintly hear the clicking of Tyler's boots, which were black with a chain running underneath the heels, echoing with the slamming lockers and noisy students decked out in their own new first-day-of-school duds.

Oh, well. I'll probably have another class with him. I'll catch him later. I'll have to let him know it's perfectly legal to dance here in Trinity Springs.

But during the rest of the morning, which included Geometry, Government and Drafting classes for Graham, he never so much as laid eyes on Tyler Nixon. He didn't even see him walking around in the halls between classes, which he thought was kind of strange.

Graham was one of the most popular students at Trinity Springs, so he wanted to make sure somebody new to the school didn't go largely ignored on his first day. Especially since Tyler was a fellow senior who would be walking the stage with them the next May.

That was the kind of thing Graham would have never put too much thought into before he lost Katy, but now he really understood the importance of being nice.

Life is just too damn short to be a dick.

As he made his way to his locker right before lunch, Graham's stomach started to growl. He opened his new locker to put his textbooks away. He also pulled out an 8x10 photo of him and Katy from prom their sophomore year from a manila folder in his notebook.

He carefully rounded a couple of pieces of tape from the small dispenser he had in his backpack, placed them on the back of the photo, and then put the picture up at eye level on the inside of his locker door.

Underclassmen at Trinity Springs High School were allowed to attend prom, mainly because the school only had about 385 students. A prom with only seniors would have barely been a small gathering.

He stared at the picture of him in his tux and purple bow tie and cummerbund and Katy in her purple, sequined dress, which again brought a smile to his face.

They were standing underneath a sign that read "Emotions in Motion," the theme of the prom, and in front of a fancy carousel prop. They both looked like there was no other place on earth they would have rather been at that moment.

Katy had that perfect look and smile on her face, which Graham transfixed on once again. He closed his eyes. He could almost smell her perfume, Christian Dior's Poison, and feel what it was like to hold her around her waist during a slow dance.

That night was also the first time he and Katy had ever had gone all the way. They were both virgins, which meant it was over really quickly, like 55 seconds tops. The second and third time lasted a bit longer.

Prom was held at a hotel, which seemed really odd to pretty much every one of the students. It was almost like school officials were suggesting all of them go ahead and have sex afterwards. Despite that, Graham and Katy did the deed in his bed.

Graham's mom was in Houston visiting her sister for the weekend, so it was the perfect opportunity that seemed like it was absolutely meant to be. Plus, the big moment was more comfortable and intimate for the both of them because of the locale.

Graham had no doubt in his mind that night he was absolutely in love with Katy. He really believed they were going to be together for a long time, even though they were still in high school. It seemed like most high school relationships usually ended prior to college.

He knew in his heart Katy was the one and that she felt the same way about him. The intimacy of sex just reinforced that notion for Graham.

They fell asleep in each other's arms early in the morning. Waking up together the next day in Graham's bed was absolutely one of the most amazing things either of them had ever experienced.

Of course, most everybody in school was aware of what had happened. Kyle knew it the instant he saw Graham's shit-eating grin the following Monday at school. Graham still had Katy's purple panties she wore that night tucked away in a safe place at home as a memento of the occasion.

"It's about fucking time," was the first thing Kyle said to him when they saw each other that Monday.

Kyle had lost his virginity a few months earlier, telling Graham about it to prepare him for when the big moment arrived. Of course, Kyle didn't bother telling him that the whole thing might clock in at a little less than a minute.

As Graham finally looked away from the photo and started to close his locker, he felt a couple of tears start to well up in his eyes. This time he fought them back as he slammed his locker door shut.

Stay strong, Graham. Stay fucking strong.

There was one decoration on the outside of his locker for being a senior and another one for being on the basketball team, which included his uniform No. 9 written in the bottom right corner.

Locker decorations were kind of a big thing at Trinity Springs High School. The cheerleaders always made them for each of the athletes, from freshmen to junior varsity to varsity, and for other extracurricular activities. Graham could tell by the lettering that Erin had meticulously penned his basketball locker decoration.

His stomach growled again, this time with much more intense volume.

Lunch time.

Graham had been looking forward to lunch all day. Most of the food in the school cafeteria sucked ass, but the cheese enchiladas were a notable exception. And, lo and behold, there those cheesy delights were on the menu for the very first damn day.

"Hell yes," Graham said when he saw the lunch menu. "That's how you start a school year!"

Trinity Springs had an open campus for lunch for juniors and seniors. There was also a Mickey D's about a mile away that made an absolute fucking mint off the students.

Graham and Kyle had eaten lunch together at McDonald's at least two or three times pretty much every week their junior year. Not today, though. Certainly not with cheese enchiladas in the offing.

"You ready for lunch?" Kyle said as he walked up to Graham near the front of the cafeteria, fumbling with his backpack to get his car keys.

"Not today, dude. Cheese enchiladas."

Kyle gave Graham the old familiar eye roll and shook his head disapprovingly. Kyle liked the cheese enchiladas, but he didn't think of them as a better alternative than taking a break from the school day and eating some fast food.

"It's your stomach. I'm getting a Quarter Pounder with Cheese, fries and the fuck out of this place for a while. See you later, bro."

"Cool," Graham said, slapping Kyle five.

Kyle headed for the front door, while Graham briskly made his way into the long cafeteria line. Graham, who regularly dressed for comfort — even on the first day of school — was sporting a basketball T-shirt that said "Trinity Springs Sidewinders" in big, block purple letters and his favorite pair of faded blue jeans.

Graham had always thought his school had a pretty cool mascot, especially since it wasn't something hyper generic like Bulldogs, Eagles or Wildcats. It seemed like every other school in Texas had one of those three damn mascots.

Shit, the other five teams in their district were all one of them. Three were Bulldogs, one was Eagles and one was Wildcats. Not exactly the peak of creativity from the old District 22-3A rivals.

The local newspaper, *The Trinity Springs Times*, often had a ball with different headlines for sports stories about the school. When they were eliminated in the Regional finals the season before, the headline in the paper the next day read: "Sidewinders' state title hopes slither away."

That, as Coach Elgin says, was some "bulletin-board material that should get you good and damn pissed off." Sure enough, that clipping hanged on the bulletin board in their locker room since the day it ran in the newspaper.

Graham was never really offended by the headline. He figured Coach Elgin would have been pissed off no matter what the headline said … even if it was "Trinity Springs loses."

But they played their asses off in that game, falling by a point to Prescott, 72-71, on a trey at the buzzer. Graham also lost a couple of nights sleep after that game. It was the deepest Trinity Springs had ever been in the playoffs in any sport. Especially since the football team was perennially good for about two wins a season and a new head coach every three years.

Graham rapidly made his way through the lunch line. He looked down at his tray, which held three steaming, gooey cheese enchiladas, pinto beans, a slice of golden cornbread, a piece of chocolate cake and a Coke.

"Hell yes," he said under his breath. "Man, Kyle does not know what he is missing."

Normally, Graham would have a small crowd at his table when he actually opted to eat in the cafeteria. This time, however, he found himself sitting all alone. He figured most of his friends wanted to avoid those awkward conversations about Katy while digging into their own delicious cheese enchiladas.

That was until Tyler Nixon came over and asked, "Hey, man, is it cool if I eat lunch with you?"

2

TYLER NIXON

"Yeah, of course, man," Graham replied as he looked completely stunned in the process of opening his Coke can. His finger was still resting on the pull tab.

Tyler pulled out a chair with his right foot. He set his tray down on the table, dropped his backpack next to the chair and plopped down before pulling up and letting out a big sigh of relief to finally take a break from the first day.

Graham was dying to take his first bite of cheese enchiladas. However, his curiosity about the new kid's story was a tad bit stronger than his hunger pangs, leaving his meal still steaming and untouched.

"It's Tyler, right?" he asked, already knowing damn well it was indeed Tyler.

Tyler Nixon, in fact — just like I jotted down on my folder in Vertigo's class.

"Yeah, that's the name they gave me," Tyler answered, as he unfolded his napkin and put it on his leg while eyeing his own plate of cheese enchiladas with more than a bit of trepidation in his eyes.

"Nice to meet you," Graham said, extending his hand. Tyler glanced up and shook it with a grip every bit as strong as Graham's. "I'm Graham Chandler."

"Yeah, nice to meet you. Mexican food in the school cafeteria. Um ... I'm thinking that's probably not a real good idea."

"No, dude, the enchiladas are actually not bad," Graham replied, careful not to oversell his favorite school lunch to the new kid." He figured Tyler would likely be extremely disappointed every other time he ate in the cafeteria.

"So, where did you move here from?" Graham asked, finally taking a sip of Coke and then cutting into his enchiladas with great gusto. "I don't think Hitch mentioned it when she introduced you to the class this morning."

"Austin. My dad got laid off from his job, so he found a new one down here. He works at the bank, lending people money and shit like that. God damn, this town is dead."

"Yeah, it is pretty boring here, but we make do with what we have. Do you play basketball or any other sport?"

Tyler laughed at that question, quickly putting down his can of Sprite to avoid spraying it all over the place.

"Hell, no! I was born without an athletic bone in my body. Coaches don't tend to like me very much, either. And the whole wearing a jock strap thing … not for me. You do, I assume? … Play sports, I mean."

"Yeah, we've got one of the best basketball teams in the state. I'm our starting shooting guard. We're winning the whole damn, um, enchilada this year. You'll have to come watch us play in your old stomping grounds and raise that trophy in the Super Drum. You can bet your ass it's gonna' happen."

"Oh, yeah? Well, that's pretty cool, I guess. I've got a few spots in town I could show you where we can get you some real damn Mexican food. I could introduce you to some pretty smoking hot chicks from my old high school, too."

Satisfied with knowing where Trinity Springs' own version of Ren McCormack was from, Graham finally tore into his beloved cheese enchiladas.

Graham thought it was pretty cool Ren drove a Beetle in *Footloose* just like he did — although his car was yellow, rather than Graham's sun-baked burnt orange.

After Graham and Tyler ate for a minute or two without any further conversation, Tyler started it back up.

"I do play guitar, though," he said while wiping the cheese from the corner of his mouth with his napkin. "I was in a band in Austin. We were called Evening Wood."

This time it was Graham who had to stop drinking his Coke as he suppressed his laughter, narrowly avoiding spraying his drink all over the new guy. Otherwise, he would have screwed up both his cool hair and his first plate of Trinity Springs High School cafeteria cheese enchiladas.

"That's so fucking awesome," Graham said after finally letting out his laughter. "That might be the coolest band name I've ever heard, Nixon. So, what kind of music do you guys play? Like Tears for Fears, U2, Men at Work?"

"Nah, man. We're more into like The Ramones and The Clash. We do a lot of covers, but we have a few originals. We do a mean 'Rock the Casbah,' if I do say so myself. The video for that song was shot in Austin, you know?"

"No shit? You write lyrics, too?"

"Nah, I totally suck with words, but I'm pretty good on guitar and help write lots of the actual music. I'm only mildly better at writing words than I am at playing sports."

"Well, you're sure to love Hitch's English class," Graham said with a smile while pointing his fork, which had another bite of enchilada resting on it, toward Tyler.

"Oh yeah, she seems like she'll be a real treat to start off my mornings. And what's with the damn homework assignment on the first day of school? Jesus."

Graham smiled as he looked down at Tyler's partially eaten plate of enchiladas and finally decided he'd pop the question: "Pretty good shit, huh?"

"Yeah, dude," Tyler said, as he chewed a big bite. After swallowing, he added, "Surprisingly good, I must admit. I sure wasn't expecting much. These are definitely pretty solid."

"Don't get used to it. The food here mostly sucks ass. Hell, they can even screw up tomato soup and grilled cheese. The cheese enchiladas are a fluke.

"Kyle and I usually go out for lunch at McDonald's instead of subjecting our stomachs to the cafeteria food, so this might be the last day I eat in the cafeteria this week."

"Kyle?"

"Oh, yeah, you'll meet Kyle soon. He's been my best friend since we were kids. He also plays basketball. He's a really funny, cool dude. You'll dig him. He's our resident jokester."

Tyler seemed to be zoning out just a little bit, like he was deep in thought about something — or maybe was just really focused on his lunch. He finally asked, "So, what exactly is it that you guys do for fun around here?"

After pondering that question for a second or two, Graham finally replied, "Well, we … we pretty much go to Austin or San Antonio."

Both of them laughed and proceeded to polish off the last of their lunches. As they did, a handful of the other seniors finally stopped at their table to say hello to Graham and introduce themselves to Tyler. Graham was happy to see his classmates being so hospitable.

Each time any of them came by, Graham thought for sure one of them was bound to say something that would force him to explain to Tyler what happened with Katy. Tyler didn't seem to know anything about the whole situation yet. And that was borderline miraculous considering if you farted at Trinity Springs High School word would get around before the air was breathable again.

After all, Tyler had all morning for somebody to give him the lowdown on the poor girl who would have been a senior right alongside him this year. Katy would most likely have been sitting with Graham and Tyler eating her own plate of cheese enchiladas, which she also loved, if she were still alive.

Somebody would surely tell the new guy all about how Katy had died in a car accident right after her junior year and how her grieving boyfriend, Graham, was putting on his fucking brave face for the first day of school.

So, you know, "Just be cool around him and try not to say anything about what happened, okay?" But, nobody so much as uttered a peep about Katy like they had all had some sort of briefing and planned it that way all along.

As the lunch period started to wind down, Erin stopped by with a couple fellow varsity cheerleaders who all seemed like they more than approved of the new kid's edgy look and certainly the fact he played guitar in a rock and roll band.

Just as he suspected in English class earlier in the morning, Graham thought Tyler was a pretty damn cool dude. He seemed like he had a good sense of humor and was the kind of guy Graham would definitely be friends with — even though he wasn't a jock.

Graham was never too concerned with cliques. He figured the school was so small there was no reason to not be inclusive of everybody.

Plus, his schoolmates were always so great about packing the gym for home basketball games and being insanely loud. So much so that Trinity Springs had not lost a varsity home game since Graham's freshman year. And the Sidewinders only lost two at home that entire season.

Unless somebody was a dick to him first, how could he possibly be a dick to people who helped give him and his teammates such a great home court advantage?

Some of the other athletes at the school didn't exactly fall in line with Graham's way of thinking. In fact, he had to get onto a couple of them a time or two for being assholes to people for no good reason.

If you weren't a jock, in their eyes, you'd better be a cheerleader or at least be in a band that plays cool music or something. Otherwise, you'd likely find yourself sitting at home every weekend, doing homework for Vertigo and dreaming of the cheese enchiladas you would eat the next time you won the cafeteria food lottery. For the most part, everybody got along really well at Trinity Springs.

Luckily for Tyler, he would have absolutely no problem scoring plenty of cool points. Graham was already convinced Tyler would surely be asked to hang out at all of the happening senior parties and to go cruising on weekends, the height of social activity if you were still in high school in Trinity Springs.

"So, what's the rest of your schedule for the day looking like?" Graham asked.

"Let's see," Tyler said, carefully taking out his schedule card and unfolding it for inspection. "It looks like Geometry, Civics and then Band to finish out the day. Whoopdee-fucking-doo."

"Band?" Graham asked, somewhat surprised. "You're in the school band, Nixon?"

"Yeah, I play a little trumpet, too. It's kind of lame, but it's something to do. I've been in marching band every year I've been in high school. We only have a few more days until the first football game. And those fucking uniforms are hot as hell. That's the only thing that thoroughly sucks about it. Like I said, it's something to do."

"You are one musical bastard. Just like Prince, huh?"

"I started taking piano lessons when I was six, and I've always loved music — especially when it's loud. And Prince is an absolute bad ass, by the way. I saw *Purple Rain* like three times in the theater. That guitar solo at the end of 'Let's Go Crazy' is beyond fucking rad. I would give my left nut — and your right one — to be able to nail that thing just one time. It's going to happen someday."

"Yeah, it is, man. I love Prince, too. I think I own every one of his tapes. They're all so damn awesome. Which one is your favorite?"

"I don't know. Maybe *Purple Rain, Controversy, 1999* ... you can't really go wrong with any of them. I got to see him play live a couple of years ago. He is fucking amazing, man. The guy plays like 27 instruments."

Tyler gave Graham a high five like they had been friends forever. As Graham finally started to pack up his tray, Tyler looked at him a bit nervously and gently grabbed the right sleeve of his T-shirt. As he did, he said in a very serious tone, "Listen, Graham, I can help you, dude."

Graham wasn't sure if he was more taken aback by Tyler grabbing his sleeve or his ambiguous comment. Graham pulled away enough to release his sleeve from Tyler's grasp.

He paused for another few seconds, staring at Tyler, before finally managing to ask, "What did you just say, man?"

"I said I can help you," Tyler repeated, with even more authority than the first time.

"What do you mean, Tyler?" Graham said in a confused but still very rational tone.

How in the fuck can this guy I just met help me with anything if he can't play basketball? We've known each other for 35 goddamn minutes.

"I can help you see Katy again. I'm completely serious, Graham. I can really make it happen."

The color started to leave Graham's face as his expression quickly turned to anger. His blue eyes were rapidly turning red. He could feel the muscles in his body stiffen up and his teeth clench in rage like a lightning bolt striking.

"Who in the fuck told you to say that?" he asked, practically yelling, which caused most of the rest of the cafeteria to begin to fall silent.

Being the main character in some big, dramatic scene was about the last thing Graham wanted to happen on this of all days.

However, he was far too pissed off to give much of a shit about his surroundings or who was listening to him at the moment. The vast majority of his classmates had never even heard Graham raise his voice.

"Graham, calm down, man," Tyler said, his voice returning to its normal tone, as he unsuccessfully tried to grab Graham's sleeve again.

"Fuck you!" Graham yelled, even louder this time, quickly pulling away from Tyler. "Who told you to say that? Tell me now or I'll kick your fucking ass right here and now in this cafeteria on the first fucking day of school, mother fucker."

By that time, every head in the vicinity of the cafeteria was turned to focus solely on what was going on between Graham and the new guy, even stopping some students in their tracks who were milling about in a nearby hallway.

"Graham," Tyler said, trying to calm him down as he was finally able to grab hold of his sleeve again. "It's okay, Graham. Just relax, man. Relax. Let me explain. That didn't come out the right way. Let's talk about it and —"

"Take your damn hand off me," Graham yelled as he pulled away from Tyler and slammed down his tray on the table, spilling the last sip of his Coke across the table. He then stormed out of the cafeteria and straight through the front doors of the school with every eyeball firmly fixated on his every step.

As he watched Graham walk away, Tyler said, "Well, that went well." He got up, gathered his things and took his tray back up to the front of the cafeteria with each and every eyeball now focused on him. You could have heard a pin drop as Tyler set his tray down and walked away.

Graham marched furiously toward his car, got in, slammed the door and loudly peeled out of the parking lot. As he did, he passed Kyle, who was coming back from McDonald's and still polishing off his large Coke refill.

Kyle did a quick U-turn, which made his tires squeal loudly, and followed Graham out onto Sidewinder Road, which was, ironically, straight as an arrow.

Kyle pulled up right behind Graham a couple of minutes later at the red light that seemingly almost never changed from red to green. Kyle joked that he once celebrated two of his birthdays while waiting for a green light at that intersection.

Graham, still shaking a little bit and breathing heavily, saw Kyle pull up behind him in his rearview mirror. When he did, Graham finally started to regain his normal calm demeanor, although his heart was still pounding in his chest like he had just finished running laps in basketball practice. For the second time in a few hours, Kyle was a sight for sore eyes.

Thank God it's Utley.

Kyle quickly jumped out of his car, a 1974 dark green Lincoln Continental with a huge Trinity Springs Sidewinders basketball sticker next to a neon green "Ultra HOT" sticker on the back window.

He approached Graham's car like he was a cop making a routine traffic stop. Kyle walked up and lightly tapped on the driver's side window.

Seeing his friend extremely upset and staring straight ahead, Kyle gave it a second or two before he even thought about giving the window another tap. While he gave pause, Kyle thought about Holly, one of the girls he met in Colorado.

The only two times he had ever seen Graham this upset were the night Katy died and one time in basketball practice when he got in a minor dust-up with a teammate.

Coach Elgin had told Graham and Richmond Bedford, the team's resident smart ass their sophomore season, to both "chill out, damn it," which quickly defused the situation because of the ridiculousness of that term coming from his mouth.

In fact, the minor scrum ended with Graham and all of his teammates laughing heartily with one another.

Of course, Richmond had started the whole thing by shoving Graham in the back on a fast break. Kyle didn't see it happen, but he knew if Graham was upset about something, somebody else must have started it.

Graham was, by far, the most easy-going, down-to-earth person Kyle had ever met. He rarely saw Graham let his emotions get the better of him.

"What's wrong, Graham?" he asked with the window still rolled up, figuring the outburst had to have something to do with Katy or maybe somebody talking shit about the basketball team or Prince. "Come on, Graham. Talk to me, dude. It's your boy, Kyle."

Graham finally looked at Kyle and obliged by rolling down his window. As he started to breathe normally, Graham told his best friend, "Go back to school, man. I'll tell you about it when we get back. I'll follow "The Big Green Machine" back. We'd better hurry, though. It's almost time for our next class."

He's got such a better nickname for his ride than I do. Rat bastard.

Graham momentarily forgot why he was so pissed off in the first place, and that he had just yelled the "F-word" about five times in the cafeteria in front of teachers and his classmates.

When they got back to school, Kyle parked, got out of his car, slammed the door and walked up to Graham's car. He plopped down into the familiar passenger seat, causing the Beetle to dip down and then bounce back up again. They only had another seven or eight minutes before the first bell for their next class, so the conversation had to be a quick one.

"What's up, Chandler? Tell me what the hell happened, bro. *Calmly* tell me what the hell happened."

Graham took a few more seconds to collect his thoughts and wipe some sweat off his brow before he finally started to speak.

"Have you met the new kid yet? Tyler Nixon."

"No, man. I didn't even know we had a new kid. Is he a senior?"

"Yes. I have English IV with him, first period. I was going to introduce myself to him this morning after class, but I wasn't able to catch up with him.

"I thought I would have another class with him today, but it turns out I don't. I already saw the rest of his schedule and English is the only class we have together."

"Weird. I haven't had a class with him so far, either — just with the same ole', same ole'. And I don't have Hitch until fifth period."

"So, anyway, this Tyler guy ends up walking up and sitting down with me at lunch. He seemed like a really cool dude at first. He sure as shit looks and dresses really cool.

"Anyway, we were just shooting the shit about what kind of music we like, how damn boring this town is — all of that stuff. We finally get done eating lunch, and the dude tells me that he can help me."

"What? Did he fucking hit on you?"

"No, dumbass, nothing like that," Graham said, lightly smacking Kyle on the arm. "I ask him what he's talking about. Then, the guy says ... get this shit ... he can help me see Katy again."

"What?" Kyle said, his voice massively increasing to almost a yell in absolute shock, much like Graham's voice had done in the cafeteria.

"What the fuck? What the hell did he mean by that? How the hell does he even know about Katy? I say we go back in there and kick his ass for that bullshit."

"I know, I know. I already told him I was going to do that. I mean, how messed up is that? Telling some dude you just met that you can help him see his dead girlfriend again? That is definite grounds for getting your ass kicked. Even if you're the new kid and it's the first day of school."

Kyle sat silently, looking completely stunned as Graham continued.

"Plus, it's just flat-out fucking weird. I don't even know how he knows anything about Katy. Or about me. And he's trying to reunite us from across the spiritual world or something? What the fuck is that all about?"

"That is completely insane. What the hell could he have meant by helping you see Katy again?"

"I don't know, but he did say he moved here from Austin."

"Oh, well, that explains a lot, huh?"

Kyle adjusted his voice to say in a countrified accent, "Only fucking weirdo hippies come from Austin way, you know, Chandler? And you damn sure can't trust nobody named Nixon. Probably been smoking dope since he was in the fourth damn grade, by God."

The two shared a robust laugh. Kyle could do about a dozen funny voices and always made Graham laugh, which was one of the reasons Graham had always liked him so much. Dude had the best sense of humor of anybody he knew, no contest.

"You should be on TV or something — just not playing basketball," Graham had often told him, which usually drew a "Very funny, Chandler. Very fucking funny," reply from Kyle.

Graham looked down at the clock on his dashboard.

12:25 p.m.

"Crap, we're going to be late for our next class. Let's motor."

They quickly exited the car, gathered their things and hopped back out into the blazing afternoon sun.

"Senior year's off to quite a start, huh?" Kyle said. "First day of class, and you've already almost gotten into a fight with the new dude and we are about to be late for class. It's good to be a senior."

"Fucking aye, Utley," Graham replied, slapping Kyle five.

Graham locked his door, saw his reflection in the glass and muttered, "Evening Wood."

"What did you say, man?"

"Nothing, Kyle. I didn't say a word."

3

DONNA ANDERSON

The longest and by far the weirdest first day of school of Graham's life was mercifully over. Although he was eager to get back home, he stopped to get some flowers to put in front of Katy's grave.

He never spotted Tyler even once the rest of the afternoon before he finished the first day up with athletics.

It had been five or six days since Graham had last been out to see Katy, which was a little longer than he typically went in between visits. He had kind of lost track of time with school starting up again and things getting busy.

After the events of the day, there was pretty much no way in hell he wasn't going to go out and visit her. He had planned to do so even before the cafeteria incident.

Katy was buried in Longview Cemetery, only a few minutes away from Graham's house. The graveyard was also less than a couple of miles from the site of Katy's accident on Farm-to-Market Road 38.

Every time Graham went to the cemetery, he passed by the scene of the wreck and saw some of the skid marks still there on the pavement. There was a cross with Katy's name written on it, flowers and an occasional stuffed animal nestled near the small embankment on the side of the road.

He had even found one of his friends leaving a memento in her honor on occasion. Graham often wondered exactly how many times he had driven by that spot without paying attention to it before he came to know it so well.

Except when he went to see Katy, he generally tried his best to avoid going near FM 38. And if it wasn't a mile-and-a-half out of the way to go a different way to visit her, he would do his damndest to never drive on that road again.

On this day, the site of the accident just sat there, still and lonely. He wasn't entirely sure who put the cross up, but it was there less than 48 hours after the wreck. He figured it was probably Katy's parents, but he never bothered to ask them.

Nearly every time he saw that awful place, he thought about what would have happened if he had been with Katy that day.

Would she still be alive? Would we both be dead?

Today was no exception as his mind wandered back to May 24. He couldn't believe it had already been three months, although in several ways it also felt like she had been gone for much longer.

Ever since Katy died, Graham found himself driving slower and wearing his seat belt every time he went anywhere — even if it was only when he went up to the E-Z Mart convenience store a few blocks from his house.

Before Katy died, Graham was somewhat prone to speeding, but he had since found himself getting passed by senior citizens on a regular basis. That is, of course, when he wasn't screeching out of the school parking lot because some new dude said he could help him see his dead girlfriend again on the first fucking day of school.

The police determined Katy was going 85 miles per hour in a 45 mph zone when she lost control of the car and crashed. Going 85 pretty much anywhere in the city limits of Trinity Springs was bonkers considering the speed limit was 50 mph or less most everywhere in town.

Graham never understood what could have possibly made her drive so damn fast that day — especially since she was so close to home. If anything, she should have been slowing down after driving on the interstate from Austin.

"Why were you going so fast, baby?" Graham said as he finally pulled his car through the gates of the cemetery a few minutes later. As usual, he drove around toward the back on the gravel road. Katy's grave was near the very back of the cemetery underneath a massive tree in section P1.

It was still blazing hot outside — at least 92 degrees with what seemed like about 150 percent humidity. It rarely got below 90 during the day until late September or early October in Trinity Springs. Texas summers don't ever end when the calendar says they should.

Luckily, his car had one seriously bad-ass air conditioner. No heater to speak of, but a seriously bad-ass air conditioner. He stopped the car, quickly got out, and then felt the wave of heat smash him in the face again like he had just opened the oven door immediately after the Thanksgiving turkey was done.

Graham walked to the front of his car, opened the trunk, grabbed the bundle of yellow roses and then slammed the trunk shut.

Being a native and loyal Texan to her very core, Katy's favorite flower had always been the yellow rose.

Most girls her age adored three things — red roses, hairspray and Bartles and Jaymes wine coolers, but that was just not Katy's style. She loved Texas, and Graham had seen her drink alcohol maybe twice, although she was also undeniably a big fan of hairspray.

The fact she adored yellow roses and her home state so much was something Graham always loved about her.

As he walked toward her tombstone, he thought about how Katy always got super excited to see the Alamo when she was in San Antonio or the state capitol when she was in Austin. And thinking of those things brought a small smile to his face. "There's no place on earth like Texas," she would frequently say to pretty much anybody who would listen.

You're right, Katy. There's no place on earth like Texas.

Katy could also tell you just about anything about Texas history from The Battle of San Jacinto to the Babushka Lady to the Von Erichs wrestling in Texas Stadium. She even had a "Come and Take It" flag hanging up in her room for the love of Willie Nelson.

Graham walked over to her headstone and stared at it for a minute or so. It read: "CHRISTOVAL" across the top and "Gone Too Soon. 1969-1986." right underneath her name. No matter how many times he stared at the tombstone, it was still so incredibly surreal. He wanted so badly for it to be a lie.

Graham knelt down and placed the yellow roses up against the headstone. He ran his fingers across her name. He closed his eyes as one tear started to stream down his cheek.

"I miss you so damn much, Katy. It was so weird at school today without you. I kept hoping this was all some crazy, fucked up dream and I would see your face and hear your laugh any second. But it's way too real."

He sat in silence for a few seconds before continuing.

"There's a new guy who told me he could help me see you again, which I know is complete bullshit. But you know I would give anything to hold you in my arms just one more time, don't you? I love you, Katy Christoval. I will always love you."

Graham bent over and gave the headstone another gentle touch with the tips of his fingers. He walked back to his car, slid in and cranked up the A/C, which immediately blew his short hair back.

As he drove to the front of the cemetery, looking back one last time in the direction of Katy's grave and at the fresh yellow roses lying against her tombstone. After wiping away a little bit of sweat from his brow, he looked left, right, left and right again before slowly pulling his car back out.

He decided to take the long way home to avoid going back on FM 38.

Once he finally got to his house, Graham pulled into the driveway to the deafening sounds of "Let's Go Crazy" blaring from his car speakers.

He thought about Tyler Nixon trying his damndest to play the guitar solo as he walked inside.

Who the fuck does this guy think he is, anyway? I mean seriously.

Graham knew he had the house to himself for at least another hour or so before his mom would be home around 5 p.m. She was one of only two dentists in Trinity Springs, so she stayed pretty busy and didn't leave her office until 4:45 p.m. most days.

Graham would jokingly tell her he didn't know how she made a living when so few people in the town had teeth. That nearly always got at least a small grin from his mom, followed by, "That's awful, Graham."

Graham figured he would go into his room, lift some weights and listen to some music on his boom box for a while before grudgingly reading *Wuthering Heights.*

Instead, he fell asleep on his bed, fully dressed, in less than five minutes. He hadn't slept worth a crap the night before, partly because he had gotten so used to staying up to all hours of the morning during the summer.

During a normal summer, he would have been hanging out with Katy and Kyle all night long. On the last Saturday before a new school year, they would usually drive out to the lake and stay up to the wee hours talking about the previous school year, the one that was about to start, and wonder what their futures might have in store for them.

Plus, Graham had always been a bit of a night owl. He hardly ever got to sleep before midnight — even when he had to get up at 7 a.m. for school the next day. He was extremely well-acquainted with his snooze button, which was yet another culprit that led to his perpetual tardiness.

This final night of this summer vacation, however, he had stayed up thinking about Katy and what it was going to be like to walk into school the next day and not see her. He tossed and turned most of the night with his mind racing.

Why Katy? Why'd she have to die so young?

Graham slept deeply for more than 45 minutes before Donna knocked on his bedroom door, finally waking him up. She knocked right above a plastic yellow sign taped to his door that read "Disaster Area," with a Trinity Springs Sidewinders basketball sticker proudly stuck to the door right underneath it.

"Honey?" she said loudly. "Honey, are you okay? Graham?"

Graham finally started to sit up in bed, wiping his face with his hands.

"Yeah, Mom. I'm good."

"Were you asleep?"

"Um, uh, no."

"Yes, you were, Graham."

"Then why did you ask me if you knew?"

"Very funny, son."

Donna smiled, rolled her eyes a little bit and headed to her bedroom to change her clothes. She was 45 years old with green eyes and brown hair that had some serious Texas elevation, with the help of her huge Aqua Net can she wielded like it was one of her dental instruments.

Even though it was a Monday night, Donna had a date. Ever since she and Miles got divorced in 1982, Donna had dated on and off. Sometimes she would see a guy for an extended period of time, but it was never for more than a few months.

In fact, five months was her dating record. The guy's name was Barry Cooper. He seemed like a cool guy to Graham the few times he had been around him, but it turned out Donna wasn't the only girlfriend Barry had. Understandably, that didn't sit too well with Donna. Or with Graham.

In fact, it really bummed Graham out because he knew she could get pretty lonely in such a small town. He really thought his parents would be married forever. They seemed so deliriously happy while he was growing up, like they could hardly stand to spend one minute away from one another. Up until Katy's death, their divorce was easily the hardest thing Graham had ever gone through.

He ended up living with Donna so that he didn't have to change schools and start all over. Donna would have fought him tooth and nail for custody of Graham anyway, but it never came to that since Miles agreed to the arrangement right off the bat.

His parents weren't in love anymore, but they still genuinely liked and respected one another. And that was more than a lot of Graham's friends could say about their parents, who seemed to be getting divorced left and right. Donna and Miles were mature about the decision the whole way.

Plus, his Dad was only a few hours away in Dallas. Graham loved visiting him at his bachelor pad apartment, but he was always ready to get back home to see his Mom and Katy again.

Miles moved to Big D right after the divorce and never left. Graham and Miles almost always caught a Texas Rangers game when Graham's visits coincided with a home stand during baseball season.

Miles would take off work early so they could get to the game in time to watch batting practice. They always had good talks about their lives on the drive to and from Arlington.

Graham's favorite Ranger was third baseman Buddy Bell. Graham loved tuning into the All-Star Game each summer to see which player represented the Rangers on the American League team. It was pretty much always Buddy.

Buddy also signed an autograph on a ball for Graham when he attended his very first Major League Baseball game. The Rangers played the California Angels at Arlington Stadium that night.

Miles told Graham that the stadium used to be called Turnpike Stadium, which Graham always thought was a really cool name. "Why did they change it again?" Graham asked his dad at least the first three or four times they went to a Rangers game.

Graham still had that autographed Buddy Bell baseball on a shelf in his room. When he was younger, he even used a magic marker to fashion his own hand-drawn Buddy Bell Rangers jersey No. 25 on a plain white T-shirt.

Miles bought him a Rangers hat, which Graham wore until it literally fell apart on his head one day. Miles immediately got him a new one, but it was never the same.

The singles scene in Trinity Springs, much like the mall, wasn't much to speak of. In fact, unless you were all about going to church, then to Luby's afterward for some fried fish, mashed potatoes, corn, a dinner roll, a slice of cherry pie and some sweet tea, then you probably weren't going to meet anybody to date without taking a trip on I-35.

Hell, the Trinity Springs High School basketball varsity home games were pretty much the biggest local events. Graham never got tired of hearing that crowd roar so loudly and feeling that adrenaline rush when the Sidewinders took the home court.

Donna typically went up to Austin or down to San Antonio to go on a date, do some shopping or to just have fun with her sister on the weekends. But driving 90 miles each way to go out on a Monday night was definitely out of the ordinary even for her.

"Honey, I'm going to Austin tonight, remember?"

Graham finally managed to roll out of bed. His clothes now completely wrinkled, he looked at himself in the mirror and rubbed his face again to try to help him wake up. He looked up at one of his bookshelves and spotted his autographed Buddy Bell baseball.

Donna had her sequined red shirt and a pair of super tight jeans lying on her bed. That was pretty much her standard first-date outfit, although she would sometimes wear her sequined blue shirt instead just to mix things up a bit.

Donna was all about the flashy, rhinestone look, and she usually got plenty of attention any time she hit the town. She sure as hell didn't resemble a woman who had a kid who was a senior in high school.

Donna had just put on her shirt and squeezed into her jeans when Graham finally stumbled into her bedroom.

"Mom, I can't believe you're going to Austin on a Monday night. You're going to be tired as hell in the morning."

"Well, I'm going into work after lunch tomorrow, kiddo. Your mom has to have some fun, you know? Besides, I'll give you some money to order a pizza. Don't you want to eat pizza, talk on the phone and watch MTV? You are a teenager, right?"

"Jesus, Mom, I am a senior in high school now, you know?"

"Yeah, I know, Graham," she said, forcing her right boot on her foot. "That's my point."

"It's just that ... just promise me you'll be careful, okay?"

"Oh, baby," Donna said as she got up. She hugged her only child and gave him a kiss, leaving him with a snoot full of perfume and a lipstick impression on his left cheek. "You know I will." She then sat back down on the end of her bed to put her other tan Roper boot on her left foot.

"How was the first day? Did everything go well?"

After pondering that question for a few seconds, Graham decided to go ahead and tell his mom what happened with Tyler at lunch.

"Pretty good — until this new kid told me he could help me see Katy again," Graham abruptly blurted out, delivering the words a lot faster than he did in his normal cadence.

Donna practically fell off the bed in shock. She didn't say anything for a moment, just looking at Graham with a mix of curiosity and disbelief in her eyes.

"I know. That was sort of the reaction I had, too. And then I told him I was going to kick his ass. It was a whole big scene in the cafeteria, Mom. Pretty much half of the school was there to witness it all."

Normally, Donna would have been majorly pissed off at the thought of Graham even entertaining the idea of getting into a fight. This time she completely understood.

"That's absolutely horrible. Somebody you just met tells you something like that? Why on earth would he do that? How does he even know about Katy? Somebody must have put him up to that. Why would he do that sort of thing, honey?"

"I don't know. What should I do, Mom? I even have a class with this dude, too — English IV, first period. By the way, my teacher in that class already gave us damn homework."

"Well, don't get in a fight, son. Why don't you let him know just how much it upset you? Then ask him why he would say something like that. Talk to him like a mature person. You're a senior in high school now, remember?"

"Um, I'm pretty sure he already knows it upset me."

"Yeah, I guess so. Still, talking it through is always the best way to resolve your problems. Getting in a fight is probably just going to get both of you hurt and in trouble. And I don't want to have to fix either of your teeth because you got in a fight. That's not like you at all, honey."

"I know, Mom. You're absolutely right."

Donna stood up, dressed to kill, and wandered over to her full-length mirror. She took a gander as she asked Graham, "How do I look, sweetie?"

"You look great ... for an old lady, I mean."

Donna rolled her eyes and handed her son a $20 bill from her purse. She grabbed her keys and quickly shuffled out the front door, once again looking to fall in love.

She thought about what the new kid had told Graham and how bizarre it was as she made her way to Austin with daylight fading. She also stayed a few miles under the speed limit — just as she had always done since Katy died.

Outside of getting passed about 50 times on I-35, going slower didn't bother her in the least. She always gave herself extra time when she travelled, so she was still 10 minutes early for her date. That was just the way she liked it, too. Unlike her only child, Donna was perpetually prompt.

Back home, Graham also thought about what Tyler had said. He thought about it while he was lifting weights in his room listening to one of his favorite tapes, Ratt's *Out of the Cellar*.

"Round and Round" blared from his boom box speakers as he did curls and managed to even sing along a bit in stunningly tone deaf fashion.

Graham also thought about Tyler's proclamation while he was eating his pizza from Domino's — pepperoni and Italian sausage with extra cheese.

And he even thought about it occasionally while he muddled through the first two chapters of *Wuthering Heights* while stretched out on his living room couch with the ceiling fan churning away on hurricane speed.

God, this book is so damn boring.

He found himself looking up several times at a framed photo of him and Katy resting on the fireplace mantle. She was smiling so big in that picture, while Graham was sweaty as hell from playing basketball. His Mom took the photo after Trinity Springs' Area playoff victory over Pearson.

Reading the work of Emily Bronte nearly put Graham right back to sleep. It was only because he already had a nap that he was able to fend off narcolepsy and keep his eyes open while struggling through the first of what he knew would be a steady dose of Hitch's homework assignments.

The worst part about it was he was just getting started with the book, although he was pleasantly surprised to discover the first two chapters were a little less than a dozen pages total.

He figured he'd be reading all night, but it only took him about an hour or so. Graham thought about getting ahead and reading Chapter 3, but after seeing that chapter was 10 pages itself, he decided patience was a virtue.

Once he was done reading, he indeed plopped down on the couch in the living room and watched MTV for a few minutes while he nursed the day's sixth Coke, fully embracing his inner teenager.

It seemed like the videos MTV was playing were all requested by one Tyler Nixon — "Rock the Casbah," "Rock and Roll High School" and "Little Red Corvette" — all consecutively.

And Tyler was spot-on about the "Rock the Casbah" video. It was filmed in Austin, which was something Graham had never really noticed before. He could clearly see City Coliseum and the state capitol in the video.

"The Clash, the Ramones and Prince," he said. "The three artists we mentioned today during our conversation today. Shit, that's kind of weird."

He looked at the clock on the wall.

10:25 p.m.

As he did, Donna slid into her 1984 black Nissan 300ZX to head home from Austin. Her car talked, which was honestly the biggest reason she bought it.

Donna and Graham were both enamored of that feature on the slick ride.

All of Graham's friends agreed it was easily the coolest car owned by any parent in Trinity Springs. Working on all of those teeth paid off big time.

Donna had a really nice time with Gregory at The Oasis. They had a spectacular view of Lake Travis as a backdrop and an incredible surf and turf dinner. The conversation was also great, which made Donna feel pretty optimistic.

Sure enough, Gregory asked her out on another date after he walked her to her car. She agreed to see him again in a week or two.

Her drive home was pretty much perfect, with hardly any traffic and a full moon hanging low in the Texas sky. She was glad she had decided to go out — even on a Monday night. She was even happier she had decided to go in late on Tuesday.

A little after midnight, Donna finally made it back to the Trinity Springs city limits. She was listening to George Strait's "Right or Wrong" on the radio when she came up on the site where Katy died.

Donna was only going 45 mph when she glanced over and saw the memorials to Katy on the side of FM 38 that Graham had driven past just a few hours earlier.

When she looked back up, there was an armadillo standing right in the middle of the road, staring her down just a few feet in front of her car.

"Shiiiiittttt!" Donna yelled at the top of her lungs as she slammed on the brakes, causing her car to slide off to the side of the road before safely coming to a stop on the embankment with no damage.

Donna sat there, stunned, as George continued to croon.

Still breathing heavily from the mild scare, she turned off the stereo and stared at the cross with Katy's name on it. She fought back tears as she looked left, right, left and then right again and gingerly pulled back out onto FM 38 with no sign of the armadillo.

She couldn't wait to get home and see Graham. Still, she did so very slowly, not even cracking 35 mph or bothering to turn the stereo back on for the short remainder of her drive.

A few miles away, Graham wandered into the bathroom to brush his teeth before turning in for the night.

As he furiously brushed, he heard his mom's car pull into the driveway and the car door slam. Any time he knew she made it back safe from a date, even before Katy's wreck, he breathed a little sigh of relief.

Donna was still gathering herself a bit after her scare as she walked into the house. She knew Graham would still be awake. She sure didn't want him to know anything about what had just happened. She just wanted to hug her son more than anything in the world.

"Hi, honey," she said, calmly as she stopped at the bathroom door and watched Graham continue to brush his teeth. "I'm back."

Graham spit out his toothpaste. "Hey, Mom. Did you have a good time?"

"It was nice. I did have a really good time. Gregory was very cool. We had a great dinner and some really nice conversation. He's a big Spurs fan, you'll be happy to know. We're going to see each other again soon. Did you get all of your homework done?"

"Yeah, I just had to read the first two chapters of *Wuthering Heights*. It wasn't as long as I thought it would be, but it still sucked Thrushcross Grange ass."

Donna gave him a quizzical look. She had no idea what he was talking about, but she was very relieved to be home again, safe and sound.

She walked into the bathroom, smiled, hugged Graham, kissed him on the forehead. "Good night, sweetie."

"Night, Mom. Love you."

Graham finished up in the bathroom and went into his room to go to bed. He walked over to his closet to figure out what T-shirt he would wear to school on Tuesday.

He saw the tuxedo he wore to the prom tucked into the garment bag on the left side of his closet. He reached out, unzipped the bag and ran two of his fingers across the tux for a moment, brushing the left sleeve as he looked at the purple boutonniere that was still pinned to the front pocket.

He closed the closet door, without picking out a shirt for the next day. Graham turned off the lights and hit the sack — this time in the T-shirt and shorts he customarily slept in.

As he was lying in bed, his thoughts quickly turned back to Katy. He remembered the first time he laid eyes on her, way back when they were in the fifth grade. He thought about how pretty she was in her ponytails. And he thought about how they hit it off right away.

Graham and Katy steadily became better and better friends before he finally got the nerve to ask her to be his girlfriend when they got to eighth grade.

"Do you want to, um, go with me?" he nervously asked her one day after school.

She smiled, grabbed his hand, kissed him on the left cheek and said, "Yes, Graham. I would very much like to go with you."

He had also found out he was going to be a starter on the Trinity Springs eighth-grade basketball team earlier that day, so he pretty much considered it the greatest day of his life. It was one of those days when everything was just so right it was almost too perfect to be real.

Even before he lost Katy, Graham rarely went more than a couple of months without thinking about that special day. When the date came up each year, it always seemed like he inevitably had a great day again, like a cosmic anniversary or something.

Kyle wasn't all that thrilled about his best friend getting a girlfriend initially, but he was eventually cool with it — especially since he got himself one a couple of months later when he started dating Erin.

Just as Graham was about to drift off to sleep, a thought popped into his head.

Katy was also a new kid. And she also moved here from Austin.

"Austin. What the hell? How did I not remember that? Damn, I can hardly fucking wait to see what happens at school tomorrow."

As Graham started to finally close his eyes and drift off, he heard his mom rustling around, getting ready for bed down the hallway.

Donna clicked off her light, closed her eyes and thanked God that damn armadillo hadn't caused her to be in a serious accident.

If, heaven forbid, something horrible had happened to her in the same exact spot where Katy died, she wasn't sure Graham would have ever been able to recover.

As always, she prayed to God to watch over Graham, but this time she also asked that he avoid getting into a fight with the new kid right before her hearty "Amen."

"If that Nixon kid messes with my son, he's going to have to answer to me," she said out loud before she closed her eyes for the night. "And you don't ever want to mess with a dentist."

4

ELSA HITCHCOCK

Unlike the first day of school, Graham was running woefully behind the second day. When he came screeching into the school parking lot, the clock on his dashboard read 7:59 a.m. He was absolutely going to be late for Vertigo's class.

"Great," he shouted. "Just fucking great."

Two mornings of his senior year, two very emphatic uses of the "F-word." Graham was shooting 100 percent.

As the final bell rang, Tyler couldn't help but notice Graham wasn't sitting in his seat. And neither could Erin.

She looked at Graham's empty chair with more than a hint of worry on her face. Especially after his profane outburst the day before, which she saw unfold from the other side of the cafeteria.

Erin was itching to have a conversation with Graham about what happened to find out exactly what Tyler had done that made him so upset.

As Tyler looked at Graham's empty chair, he wondered if his absence had anything to do with what had happened on Monday. Erin noticed him looking at Graham's chair and shot him a disapproving glance, which went completely unnoticed by Tyler.

Erin could not imagine what Tyler could have said to set Graham off, when just a couple of minutes beforehand, Graham and Tyler were talking like they were old friends.

Mrs. Hitchcock barely got the words, "Okay, class," out before the front door wildly flung open, causing everybody in the room to stop and look directly at Graham. He scurried inside and quickly found his way into his squeaky chair.

He ran all the way from his car, through the parking lot and into the building in a little more than one minute, so he was barely late. Graham thought that might help him possibly avoid a tardy slip this time — especially so early in the school year. He thought wrong.

Mrs. Hitchcock was anything but impressed with Graham's obvious effort to hurry to first period. In fact, she promptly went to her desk, filled out a tardy slip and dropped one of the familiar yellow pieces of paper on Graham's desk as he started to pull out his copy of *Wuthering Heights*.

"Oh, my God … really?" Graham pleaded. "Come on! I'm only a minute or two late, Verti … I mean, Mrs. Hitchcock."

"Late is late, Mr. Chandler, whether it's one minute or 25 minutes. It's the second day of school, for heaven's sake. … Besides, I've always been more of a *North by Northwest* fan, personally."

The rest of the class laughed as Graham shot her a go-straight-to-hell look.

He took his tardy slip, folded it in half and tucked it away in his notebook. The front pocket of his notebook each year had become his usual home for tardy slips.

Graham had probably broken the school record for being late at Trinity Springs High School. Every time he got three tardy slips, the result was a trip to after-school detention hall, which was basically an extra 90 minutes of incarceration.

Graham had completely lost count of how many times he was home from school late because he had been sitting in detention until 4:30. His mom even occasionally beat him to the house.

Of course, Graham managed to get his act together during basketball season so he wouldn't miss practice after school or, heaven forbid, a game. Kyle had taken to altering the term D-Hall to G-Hall in honor of Graham's consistent visits. Graham found that every bit as amusing as he did "The Nazi Mobile."

"I'm surprised you don't have a patch on your letter jacket for detention," Katy once joked with Graham after a particularly impressive tardy streak of four straight days. "Quit busting my balls," Graham replied as they laughed and hugged.

But, Katy often wrapped up one-act play practice while he was finishing up G-Hall in the spring semester of their junior year, so it worked out pretty well. Otherwise, he'd have to wait around and watch play practice for an hour before he could give her a ride home.

He was so proud of Katy for trying acting, which she had never done until she landed the role of Eliza Doolittle.

Her friends encouraged her to give acting a shot. She was reluctant, but she finally caved and ended up extremely happy she did. Graham knew if even half of Katy's personality came across on stage, she would be absolutely amazing. He was right.

Katy truly loved the play, as she caught the acting bug and even started pondering the idea of making theater her major or minor once she started college. Prior to the one-act play, she had no idea what she wanted to study after she graduated from high school. She just knew it would be at a college somewhere in Texas.

Another big reason for her enthusiasm was the fact Trinity Springs won state in one-act play. Katy was also named Best Actress at the competition in Austin.

Graham started to look around the classroom, mainly to avoid making eye contact with any of his classmates.

Come on, Hitch. Let's get this show on the road.

Like lots of teachers, Mrs. Hitchcock's room was full of wall decorations. Most of the decorations were laminated copies of book covers, like *The Scarlet Letter, Anna Karenina, The Great Gatsby* and the dreaded *Wuthering Heights.*

But, there were also select passages, poems and sonnets from other works on the wall that were among her favorites. Hitch had a small

Texas state flag hanging up in the back of the room, which Graham knew Katy would have loved if she had been there to see it.

"Did everybody read the first two chapters of *Wuthering Heights?*" Mrs. Hitchcock asked, glancing toward the poster on the wall that showed the book's cover. The entire class gave her an unenthusiastic "yes" that was much closer to being in unison than on the first day.

Unfortunately.

Mrs. Hitchcock had heard from several of her colleagues about how perpetually late Graham was to class. She aimed to let him know right off the bat she wasn't going to put up with that kind of crap from him or any of his fellow seniors.

Seniors always seemed to get more and more lackadaisical the deeper they got into the school year. She aimed to set the tone, so she decided to also call on Graham first for his opinion on the first homework assignment.

"Graham, why don't you tell us what you thought about the first two chapters of the book? Come on. Stand up in front of the class. Chop, chop."

Feeling even more annoyed, Graham looked at her before he grudgingly got up, having finally caught his breath from his unplanned morning sprint. His eyes wandered and made contact with Erin, and then with Tyler. He wiped a trickle of sweat off his brow.

His mind was racing, but he had to somehow come up with something to say, other than: *The first two chapters of this old-ass book by some old-ass English chick really sucked ass!*

Any book that started with "1801" instantly made Graham start to lose life force. He wasn't exactly big on classic literature or, really, much of any literature, for that matter — unless it was a Stephen King book.

Any time Graham had to do a book report with his choice of subject matter, it was inevitably one of Stephen King's. He figured he had read at least 10 of his novels. When he read them, he always wondered what it would be like to live way up in Maine, like Stephen King, and be able to write for a living. *Firestarter, Pet Sematary, Salem's Lot, Cujo,*

Carrie, Christine. He knew and loved each and every one of them. He had even read a couple of them twice.

Graham slowly made his way to the front of the classroom, again sporting a T-shirt and faded blue jeans.

He stood behind the lectern, glanced at Mrs. Hitchcock and began to speak. "Well, to tell you the truth, I thought it was kind of boring. I mean, who cares about some dude renting some house in England, right? I hope it gets better, but I'm really not feeling very optimistic about it so far. And seriously … 1801?"

That drew a boisterous laugh from everybody in the classroom. Well, almost everybody. Although she was certainly not amused, Mrs. Hitchcock was a little surprised by the candor of Graham's answer. She was even more surprised he actually seemed to have done his assignment.

For some reason, she had pegged Graham as the kind of student to blow off a first homework assignment of the year. He was actually pretty good about keeping up with his studies, because he couldn't risk failing a class during basketball season. Not to mention, his Mom would have made his life miserable if he failed a class any time of the year.

"Well, Graham, the author is setting up the plot. She's introducing you to some of the characters. Don't you think you might want to give the book more of a chance than just a couple of chapters? It really does get better, I promise."

"I guess so. It's just so old and boring. And I'm not real big on ghost stories, either."

Coming from Graham, that comment almost made Mrs. Hitchcock fall out of her chair. It also drew a gasp or two from a couple of his classmates, although he hadn't meant it like that at all. Graham realized what he had said and turned a little bit red as he suddenly felt uncomfortable standing in front of his classmates.

Mrs. Hitchcock's sympathy for Graham instantly overrode her need to try to continue to make an example of him. She decided he had had enough and let him off the hook.

Mrs. Hitchcock never had Katy in any of her classes, but she knew her a little bit. The two of them struck up a conversation or two in the halls from time to time after Katy started one-act play.

Unlike Graham, Katy liked to read, so she and Mrs. Hitchcock had talked about some of the books that would be assigned to the class to read in English IV. Mrs. Hitchcock remembered Katy specifically telling her during one of their chats she was looking forward to reading *Wuthering Heights*.

Mrs. Hitchcock, who taught four English IV classes and journalism, had also complimented Katy on her performance in the one-act play.

Graham couldn't go to the state competition because it was on a school day. He would have just skipped class if he hadn't had two big tests that day, and he was really upset that he couldn't make it. However, he also thought Katy might not be quite as nervous without him watching from the audience.

Mrs. Hitchcock could still see Katy's pretty face and bright smile clearly in her mind. It was the first time in her teaching career a student at her school had died, which had really shaken her up pretty badly.

She couldn't imagine what it would be like had she actually taught Katy in a class and had known her even better.

There really weren't too many people at the school — students or teachers — who weren't affected by Katy's death. And even three months later, the shock was still in the process of wearing off for most everybody. The new school year without her there made that grief incredibly palpable.

"Okay, Graham, you can sit down now," Mrs. Hitchcock said in an uncharacteristic hushed tone. "Anybody else have any impressions of the first two chapters?"

Graham walked back to his seat and couldn't believe his ears when he heard Tyler say in his booming baritone voice, "Yeah, I've got some impressions."

Tyler was dressed sharper than pretty much anybody else in the school once again. This time, he was wearing a Prince T-shirt, acid washed jeans and the same black boots he wore on Monday.

Tyler stood out from his classmates, but not in a way that was alienating or weird. More than anything, he was just an enigma because he was new and had clearly done something to piss off Graham, who pretty much never got pissed off, right out of the chute.

Tyler looked like he could have been playing guitar in a video on MTV, instead of just watching it religiously like the rest of his classmates. As hard as he tried, Graham just could not imagine Tyler in a marching band uniform. He couldn't wait to see what the new kid would look like on Friday night at the first football game with his spiked hair hidden by one of those enormous band hats with a feather on top.

As Tyler got up to speak, Graham made the decision he would definitely heed his Mom's advice and try to calmly talk to the new kid after class about what had happened the day before.

Sure, Graham was initially as pissed off as he had ever been. But, he was also incredibly curious about what Tyler had meant when he said he could help him see Katy again. It had to be complete crap, but Graham wanted to know how he found out about Katy in the first place. Curiosity was definitely getting the better of him.

"This story, so far, is a lot like a double album," Tyler began. "You have to give it a chance to breathe, and then really soak it in to appreciate it for everything it is — like Pink Floyd's *The Wall* or The Beatles' White Album. It's a marathon, not a sprint, you know? I don't know if it will be great like those albums, but I guess I'm just saying it's too early to tell."

Tyler paused and surveyed the room. He cleared his throat and continued …

"It's like judging the whole thing by only the first couple of tracks. You have to hear it all the way through and judge it as a whole. After all, it just might end up being a real classic, right?"

That drew some snickers from a classmate or two, but Tyler firmly believed in what he was preaching about the music that he loved. Tyler wasn't much of a reader, either, but he certainly appreciated good art of any kind.

He also pretty much drew comparisons to music for almost everything in his life. Graham was more than a little pleasantly surprised to hear a sports metaphor — even if it had nothing to do with basketball — coming from Tyler's mouth.

"I'm serious," Tyler continued before Mrs. Hitchcock could even respond. He looked over at Graham and continued, "Not every first impression is the right one. I mean I didn't even like *Combat Rock* all that much the first time I heard it. Can you imagine that?"

The rest of the class laughed again. Mrs. Hitchcock finally cut Tyler off, having heard enough of his early assessment of *Wuthering Heights* and double albums. She didn't know Tyler well enough to tell whether or not he was clever enough to reference English bands while talking about a book by an English author. It was probably just a coincidence.

After discussing the book further with the class for the ensuing 40 minutes, she assigned the next three chapters of the book to be read by Friday, drawing a chorus of groans from her largely disinterested students.

"Come on, guys. It's a tad bit early to have a case of Senioritous, isn't it? We're just getting started with the school year. Fear not. Christmas break is right around the corner. It will be here before you all know it."

For Graham, first period had dragged by especially slow, mainly because he was so eager to talk to the new kid after class. Graham could hear Katy's voice singing "Footloose" in his head during the eternal last couple of minutes of English IV.

When the bell finally rang, Graham made a beeline to Tyler, which took the old doppelganger of Ren McCormack aback a little bit.

He probably thinks I'm about to deck him in the mouth.

Erin gave the duo a curious look, not at all expecting to see them in such close proximity to one another, as she shuffled out of the classroom. She glanced back at Graham, smiled and waved goodbye, hoping that might help him maintain at least a little bit of his cool.

Had she not been in a hurry to stop by her locker to get a book for her next class, she would have stayed behind for a couple of minutes to find out what exactly was going on. Soon it was just Graham, Tyler and Mrs. Hitchcock remaining in the classroom.

After giving Vertigo a quick glance, Graham leaned against one of the empty desks and said to Tyler quietly, "Hey, man. I'm sorry I lost my temper yesterday. You really caught me off guard, though. Way, way the hell off guard."

Tyler smiled and, with relief in his voice, said, "No, dude. I sprung that on you all wrong. I shouldn't have just come right out with it like that. I just couldn't come up with any good way to say it, you know? I told you I totally suck with words. That's my bad."

Mrs. Hitchcock couldn't help but overhear a little bit of the conversation. She decided to interrupt. "You boys better get to your next class. You don't want another tardy slip on the second day of school, do you, Mr. Chandler? Or have you been pining for detention over the summer?"

"No, ma'am. And no, ma'am."

Graham looked at Tyler and said, "We'll talk later, okay?" He held out his hand for Tyler to shake. Tyler grabbed his hand, shook it firmly and said, "Cool."

Tyler started toward the classroom door. Graham followed, but Mrs. Hitchcock stopped him by reaching out and grabbing the sleeve of his T-shirt — almost exactly like Tyler had the day before at lunch. She intentionally waited until Tyler was out of earshot before speaking.

"Graham, I just wanted to tell you how sorry I am about Katy. She was a very sweet girl, from what little I knew of her, and a damn good actress. I think I speak for the entire faculty when I say she was very well thought of at this school. And you can come and talk to any of us any time you need to."

"Thanks, Mrs. Hitchcock. That's very nice of you to say. That means a lot to me — it really does. I sure wish Katy was here with us right now."

"I do, too, Graham. I can't imagine any parent or boyfriend having to endure that kind of loss. She was so young ... such a tragedy. You keep your chin up, okay?"

She then moved directly back into teacher mode. "And make sure you do your reading assignment by Friday. There just might be a pop quiz or something like that you might want to be ready to take."

"I will, Mrs. Hitchcock. See you tomorrow. And thanks."

After Graham left, Mrs. Hitchcock was all alone in her silent classroom. Second period was once again her free period for the fall semester. She usually spent her free period reading, grading tests or papers, eating a late breakfast or, if she had time, getting in some walking.

She typically had coffee, a bagel and a piece of fruit for her breakfast. On Friday, she'd usually splurge and eat a cinnamon roll or a doughnut.

However, Graham's comment about ghost stories and thinking about Katy had completely thrown her off her routine. Instead of walking to the teachers' lounge to get her breakfast out of the refrigerator, she got up from her desk and started to meander around her classroom.

She wandered to the back of the room and looked down at some of the books nestled in the small, two-level bookshelf built into the wall.

On the bottom shelf sat each of the Trinity Springs yearbooks from the first five years she taught at the school. She reached down and grabbed her copy of the 1985-86 *Rattler*. Even though the yearbook included every student in every grade level in the school district, it checked in at a modest 192 pages.

Elsa sat down in the nearest desk to her and started to slowly thumb through the yearbook. She stopped on page 18, where she spotted a photo of Graham and Katy sitting together in the hallway, working on their homework assignments.

One of the more unusual things about Trinity Springs High School was that all four main hallways — one for freshmen lockers, one for sophomore lockers, one for junior lockers and one for senior lockers — were fully carpeted. Elsa always felt a bit sorry for the school's lone custodian, who had to vacuum those huge-ass hallways late every afternoon.

But the students loved the hallways because they could sit in them and hang out when they weren't in class. The carpet seemed to create even more of a communal vibe for each grade level, although there was never a shortage of grab-ass going on in the hallways, either.

Both Katy and Graham had big smiles on their faces in the photo taken in the junior hallway, making sure they were cheesing especially hard for the camera. They looked so sweet together, Elsa thought. Both of their faces were lit up like Christmas trees.

Katy was wearing Graham's black and purple letter jacket with a big "TS" in block letters and a small basketball in the bottom right corner of the "S" on the front. The jacket had plenty of patches on it, none of which were for detention hall for the record. On the back, "Chandler" was written in cursive.

Graham was wearing a blue and green Coca-Cola shirt, rather than his usual, standard-issue TSHS basketball T-shirt, and a Swatch watch in the picture, Elsa noticed. Graham only owned about three or four collared shirts, so seeing him wear one in an unplanned yearbook photo was a pretty sizable upset.

Although she couldn't be 100 percent sure, Elsa thought she remembered the very day that photo was taken. She was almost positive it was toward the end of the fall semester, which was not too long before Katy tried out for the one-act play.

Looking at the picture made the fact that Katy was dead even more difficult to believe because she was so full of life in that photo. Elsa stared at the picture for another few seconds before she continued flipping through the small annual, which was about half the size of most yearbooks that were only for high schools.

On Page 36, she saw another photo of Graham and Katy dancing together at prom, underneath the big "Emotions in Motion" banner.

Once again, they looked like they could not have possibly been any happier than they were in that moment. Elsa also loved the fact Katy's dress and Graham's tie and cummerbund were Trinity Springs High School purple.

Sporting school colors, she thought. Of course.

Then, she reached the sports section of the yearbook. Elsa looked for a second at the football pages in the front of the section before quickly flipping over to boys basketball. That section was the one she fully intended to go to when she sat down with the *Rattler* in the first place.

The biggest photo in the entire sports section was on Page 72. Elsa practically had the path to that page memorized without even looking, having gone to it at least a couple dozen times. She had been to that page so much that it was noticeably more worn than the other pages in the yearbook.

In that sizable photo, Vernon Wylie was putting up a shot in the Regional championship game. But Elsa's eyes always went directly to the left of Vernon where Coach Abbott Elgin was standing with his eyes trained on Vernon and arms outstretched in the air.

Every time she saw that picture of Abbott, she couldn't stop herself from smiling if she tried.

She fixated on the picture. Even though there was a portrait of Abbott two pages later, it was that photo of him the she truly adored.

He was in the heat of battle, wearing his collared shirt and khakis with bright white sneakers that always looked brand new. She often wondered how long he worked to get his shoes so white before games.

Elsa thumbed through the yearbook for a few more minutes before she finally returned it to its spot on the bookshelf, kicking up some a small poof of dust.

She looked up at the clock.

9:20 a.m.

She was surprised she had been sitting there thumbing through the yearbook for such a long time. On cue, her stomach let out a small growl, eager for some breakfast.

As she made her way back to her desk at the front of the room to go get a quick bite before third period, she was drawn into her favorite piece of literature in the entire classroom. It was Shakespeare's Sonnet No. 57.

She stopped and ran her hand across the laminated piece of blue paper hanging on the wall with the sonnet printed on it in large letters. She began to read aloud, although she had memorized that sonnet long ago, when she was a student at Stephen F. Austin State University in Nacogdoches.

> "*Being your slave, what should I do but tend*
> *Upon the hours and times of your desire?*
> *I have no precious time at all to spend,*
> *Nor services to do, till you require.*
> *Nor dare I chide the world-without-end hour*
> *Whilst I, my sovereign, watch the clock for you.*
> *Nor think the bitterness of absence sour*
> *When you have bid your servant once adieu;*
> *Nor dare I question with my jealous thought*
> *Where you may be, or your affairs suppose,*
> *But like a sad slave, stay and think of nought,*
> *Save, where you are how happy you make those.*
> *So true a fool is love that in your will*
> *Though you do anything, he thinks no ill.*"

After reading the sonnet a second time, she turned around, walked back to her desk and sat down. Elsa glanced at the sonnet hanging on the wall once more.

Before she had even read #57 for the umpteenth time, she knew those words had never applied to her life more than they did at that very moment. She knew in her heart Abbott didn't feel the same way about her as she felt about him.

5

ERIN MANSFIELD

The most glorious sound of any school day — the final bell — rang out loudly, immediately causing much rejoicing at Trinity Springs High School.

Classroom doors flung open and the carpeted hallways rapidly filled with students either rushing to their lockers to put away their books for the day or heading straight to the parking lot. Some of them were talking about the day, while others were listening to their favorite cassette tapes on their Walkmans.

Erin Mansfield packed up her black and white checkerboard backpack. She walked out of her last class and headed straight towards her locker to put away some books she didn't need.

Wearing a Trinity Springs cheerleading T-shirt, she had just arrived at her locker when she spotted Graham heading toward his own, just five lockers down.

It had been one of the many days since May that Erin had spent most of her time thinking about Katy — mostly because certain places at school reminded her so much of spending time with her best friend.

In her mind, Erin could still see Katy walking the halls, smiling and laughing or holding hands with Graham as he walked her to class.

So much so that at one point earlier in the day, right before lunch, she did a double take because she could've sworn she had seen Katy briskly walking toward the theater.

Erin quickly realized her mind was just playing tricks on her, although it shook her up a bit.

In the last few hours of the afternoon, Erin thought about all of the times she and Katy went outside, behind the school, to eat lunch and soak up some rays on sunny days.

She thought about when they would goof off in gym class and talk about all of the boys in school and which one of them Erin should date. And she thought mostly about the library, where Erin was an aide her junior year.

She vividly remembered Katy excitedly rushing into the library to tell her she had landed the lead in the one-act play, causing pretty much every person studying in the library to abruptly look up from what they were doing.

She was so excited about playing Eliza Doolittle. Of course, Erin was equally as excited to hear the news. They had to go into one of the library offices and shut the door so Katy could tell her all about it without further disturbing everybody else.

"You're going to be on the front row when we perform the play for the school, Erin," Katy had said emphatically. "You have got to be there for me!"

"Wild horses couldn't keep me away," Erin told her as she hugged Katy again. And she was true to her word. She was front row center for the school performance.

Erin was so proud of how hard Katy had worked at learning her lines and was ecstatic the play won state. She wanted to go to the state competition to see them perform, but Erin had the same two classes as Graham with big tests.

It just wasn't meant to be for either of them to be there to watch her. But they had both been to all of the previous competitions, so they got to see the play several times.

Katy doing a Cockney accent was about the greatest thing Erin had ever heard — especially from the front row of the Trinity Springs High School Theater. Erin spent most of the 40 minutes laughing heartily and trying to make sure she didn't mess Katy up. She knew from the first time she saw a rehearsal Katy was really, really good.

The afternoon the cast performed the play for the entire school there was an assembly in the morning to celebrate their Class 3A state championship. It was the first time Trinity Springs had ever won state in one-act play. In fact, it was the school's first state title in any competition in decades.

That day was also one of the best of Katy's life. Graham was beaming with pride, standing there in the corner of the gym watching her wave to the school with her gold medals draped around her neck. Graham thought she looked a lot like Kim Novak in *Vertigo*.

Katy noticed Erin's exuberance at the school performance, but she handled it like she had been on the stage her entire life. Even though it wasn't a competition, Katy was all business when it came to the show any time they performed. She took her commitment to playing Eliza Doolittle very seriously.

Erin wished she had a nickel for every time she heard Katy rehearsing her lines while they were hanging out together. She even started to hear Katy say, "The rain in Spain falls mainly on the plain," in her sleep.

Without saying a word, Erin walked over to Graham and reached out to hug him. As she wrapped her arms around him tightly, she lost control of her emotions and began crying on his shoulder, drawing glances from the handful of students still lingering in the hallways.

Of course, they all immediately knew why Erin was upset. Graham just held her tightly and patted her on the back as they embraced and a few of her tears ran down his sleeve.

"I miss her so much," Erin sobbed. "Why did she have to go so soon, Graham?"

"I don't know, Erin. I really don't know."

Suddenly, Graham couldn't hold back his tears any longer and they began to stream down his face. He quickly let go of her with one of his hands to wipe his tears away.

They hugged for another few seconds before Erin let go and said, "I'm so sorry, Graham. It has just hit me really hard today, you know? I was thinking about all of the times we had talking to each other in the library and eating lunch outside. Just seeing those places again without her brings back so many memories. I think it somehow makes her not being here seem more real."

"Believe me," Graham said in an empathetic tone, "I know. Her not being here these first two days has been so surreal. Don't you ever hesitate to talk to me about it, Erin. I'm here for you any time. You were damn sure there for me.

"Shit, I'll probably need you to be there again for me another hundred times or so this year. It's okay to let it out, you know? It would be much worse if we held it all inside."

That made Erin smile a little bit as she also wiped the tears from her eyes and worried about her makeup running.

Graham had decided earlier in the day he would also tell Erin about what Tyler had told him at lunch the day before after school. He figured she was probably dying of curiosity like everybody else.

He considered for a bit that it might not be the best time to spring all of that on her since she was already so upset. However, Graham knew Erin would hear him out and probably give him some of the best advice he could get from anybody, so he decided to go ahead and tell her.

Erin had always been the voice of reason of their tight-knit group of friends. She knew what to say in nearly every sticky situation, which often kept the rest of them from doing really dumb things and getting in trouble.

Graham had figured out a long time ago Erin was incredibly smart. He expected that, like his Mom, she would tell him not to get into a fight with Tyler, and just hear what the new guy had to say.

She would probably tell him that it wasn't worth it to get into a fight over, which he already knew was true.

"Listen," he said, with the hallways nearly empty, "I'd like to talk to you for few minutes this afternoon."

"Sure."

"Why don't we go over to my house? I want to be alone when I tell you what I've got to say. I've got athletics in a few minutes. Could you meet me at my house in an hour-and-a-half?" She agreed to meet Graham at his house around 4:45 p.m.

After going home to put her backpack away and relax for a while, Erin pulled up to Graham's house at 4:43, three minutes before he did.

Seeing Erin's 1986 maroon Mercury Cougar parked in his driveway made Graham recall the night he, Katy, Kyle and Erin piled into that car and drove down to San Antonio for a Spurs game the day after Christmas.

Their tickets for the game were obstructed view seats at HemisFair Arena, so they spent most of the game trying to watch around a huge beam that seemed like it was practically down the center of their aisle.

"Well, the tickets do say obstructed view," Erin pointed out to Graham. They laughed all the way home thinking about their "great" seats. But at least the Spurs beat the Lakers, 109-91, so Graham and Kyle were happy.

Of course, Katy made Erin drive past the Alamo before they got back on I-35 to head home. Erin knew that request was coming after they didn't have time to do so before the game.

Although they had dated for a very short time in junior high, Kyle and Erin had really become pretty good friends. And they always had a good time hanging out with each other and with their best friends — especially on a road trip.

Kyle had informed Graham after he and Erin broke up, "She's just too hot, man. I always feel like every dude is drooling over her everywhere we go — even the older dudes in high school. It's kind of weird. Plus, I can't date one chick for too long. You know that, Chandler."

Graham got out of his car and greeted Erin in his driveway. He was already focusing on what he was going to tell her and hearing her reaction, so his face suddenly turned very serious again to set the tone.

"Come on in," he said.

Erin followed Graham into the house and into the kitchen. He grabbed two Cokes for them before they plopped down on the couch.

Graham was strictly an old-school Coca-Cola guy. That New Coke shit didn't fly with him at all. He also grabbed a couple of nacho cheese Corn-Quistos from a bag in the pantry, offered Erin some, and then proceeded to munch on a few before he started to speak.

Both of them opened their drinks and took sips. Graham set his Coke on a coaster on the coffee table and finally opened up to Erin about Tyler Nixon and the "cafeteria incident."

"So, you remember coming over and introducing yourself to the new kid from our English class yesterday at lunch?" Graham asked.

"Of course I do. It's Tyler, right? Didn't he move here from Austin? He plays in a band, right?"

"Yeah, Evening Wood. Pretty cool and funny name, I must say."

"That is pretty funny. So, what the hell happened? What did he say to you yesterday? I've never heard you yell like that, Graham. Was it about Katy?"

"Yeah, it was. We were starting to get to know each other at lunch. He was telling me all about playing in the band and that he doesn't play any sports. You know, small talk, mostly. Then, this dude says, totally out of the blue, he can help me see her again."

Graham thought his Mom was shocked when he told her about what Tyler had said; Erin was practically catatonic. So much so that Graham reached out and snapped his fingers in front of her face, saying her name to bring her back.

"Erin. Earth to Erin."

She finally looked at Graham as a couple of tears fell from her eyes again. He reached out and dutifully wiped them away, gently tapped her on her right cheek and gave her his best attempt at a smile.

"What in the hell is that supposed to mean?" she asked with a hint of anger in her voice and her eyes trained on Graham's face.

Erin was the nicest person Graham had ever known, so it was a tone he wasn't sure he'd ever heard before. He suspected Erin, given the opportunity, would have gladly helped him kick Tyler Nixon's ass at that very moment.

"Good question. I really don't know, but I'm going to find out. I told him after Hitch's class this morning that I wanted to talk to him about it."

Erin continued listening as she tried to process everything Graham was saying.

"When he said he could help me see Katy yesterday, I told him I was going to kick his ass, as I'm sure you heard. I thought a lot about it last night. And I talked to Mom about it. I want to at least find out what he meant. I mean, the dude doesn't know me from Adam and hits me with that shit, bam … right off the bat."

Graham looked Erin in the eyes to gauge what she was thinking before he continued. She still looked extremely puzzled and angry.

"Plus, he actually seems like a pretty good dude. He must have a reason to say that to me, right?

"We were going to talk this afternoon, but somebody told me he left school after third period because he got sick or something. It's all just so fucking weird, Erin. I've been trying to make sense of it since yesterday. It's pretty much all I've thought about. I don't know what would have made him say it, but I really think it is total crap."

Erin sat silent. She glanced over at the same picture of Katy and Graham on the fireplace mantle he had studied the night before as the ceiling fan churned. She thought about what to say before speaking.

"I don't know, Graham. You might not want to even know what he meant by it. It sounds to me like this guy is playing some sick joke on you or something like that. I think it's ridiculous. He didn't even know Katy. How could he possibly help you see her again?"

"I know, but the guy goes to school with us. He's in our damn English IV class for God's sake. It's not like I can just forget about it and ignore him for the rest of the school year. He's going to be there every single day, you know?

"And it's a long way until graduation. I think it will be better for both of us to go ahead and talk about it and get it all out there in the open. Then, we can move forward."

"I hadn't really thought of it that way. I guess that makes sense. Just don't let this guy mess with your mind, okay? Just listen to what he says and try to figure out why he would say something stupid like that to you if he doesn't explain his logic.

"I do think you're right, though. I'm guessing once you sit down with him to talk to him, he'll probably just tell you that he was screwing around with you and that will be that."

"The other thing is … what if, on a very off chance, he's not bullshitting me? What if he really can help me see Katy again? You know, with some supernatural crap or something like that? I mean, it's not at all likely, I know. But there's a chance…"

Erin interrupted, "Graham, come on. You know as well as I do there is no way that's possible. That's just some kind of made-up stuff you see in a movie or something.

"I know you would give anything to see her again — to have a chance to really say goodbye to her. So would I … in a heartbeat. But I don't think you should get your hopes up. She's gone, Graham. She's never coming back. I know how hard that is to hear, but you know it's true. We have to accept it."

"Yeah, I know," Graham said, taking another sip of his Coke. "I guess I'm just more curious than anything about what he has to say. If you've got the balls to say something like that to somebody you just met, there must be a good reason."

Erin felt like she was about to cry again, but this time she managed to fight back her tears. She stood up and told Graham she had to get home.

"I've got a crap load of homework tonight. And I've got to figure out how to squeeze in some reading, too. If I blow it off tonight,

I'll end up staying up late Wednesday and Thursday night reading *Wuthering Heights* for Mrs. Hitchcock."

"Me, too," Graham said, also getting up from the couch. "I have a ton of stuff to do tonight. That reminds me — Hitch hinted to me we will probably have a pop quiz about the book on Friday."

"Thanks for the heads up."

Graham put his arm on Erin's right shoulder.

"Thanks for coming over, Erin. I'll let you know what Tyler says when I get around to talking to him. Hopefully, he'll be back in school tomorrow. It's been such a weird start to the school year already. And we're only two days in."

"Call me if you need anything."

"You know I will," Graham said, giving Erin another quick hug. "Come on, I'll walk you out to your car."

Almost like Erin could tell what Graham was thinking, she asked him as they approached her car, "Remember when we all went to the Spurs game? We thought we were pretty big stuff going to San Antonio all by ourselves for the first time.

"I remember you and Kyle trying to see who could eat the most cheese enchiladas at Sombrero Rosa. And those big-ass poles in our way once we got to the Spurs game? God, that was hilarious. You were so mad because you bought us the tickets and it was so hard to see around them."

"Yeah, we're on the same wavelength, Erin. I was just thinking about that night when I pulled up and saw your car. That was such a great time. You remember singing 'Hungry Like the Wolf' and 'Hot For Teacher' the last few miles on the way home?"

"I couldn't possibly forget that. I still think about it every time I hear those songs. And I still have my ticket stub from that game. It's tucked into the corner of my bedroom mirror.

"When I think about Katy, that's one of the times I remember most. It makes me smile to think about seeing you two together at that game. You were so sweet to her, Graham. You kept asking her if she wanted anything to drink and if she could see okay, which, of course, she couldn't because those damn poles were in the way. She loved you so much. She really did."

"I know she did. I loved her, too. I still do — very, very much."

Once Erin got back home, she walked into her bedroom and walked directly over to her mirror to look at her Spurs ticket stub, which featured an outline of the Alamo. She reached up and pulled down the ticket so she could hold it for a few seconds.

She then walked to her bookshelf, grabbed her copy of the 1985-86 *Rattler* and started to thumb through the yearbook, just like Mrs. Hitchcock had done earlier in the day.

Unlike her English teacher, she went directly to the junior class individual pictures to look at Katy and Graham's portraits. She looked at each of them for a couple of minutes, running her fingers across both photos.

Then, she flipped to the final few pages, where several of her classmates had signed their names and written brief messages to her the day they got their yearbooks, near end of the school year.

On the first page of signatures, right after the index, Erin stopped to read what Graham had written in blue ink in the top left corner:

> Erin,
> I can't wait for you to cheer us on to a state championship next year. We're going to beat Prescott and get to Austin — count on it. Then, Katy and I will both have state championships! I can't believe we're going to be seniors. You are a great friend I am so lucky to have. Class of '87 rules!
> Love,
> Graham Chandler #9

Underneath his signature, which Graham had spent months perfecting when he was in eighth grade, he had drawn a small heart with "GC + KC" written on the inside. It was typically the kind of thing you would see the girlfriend in the relationship do, but Graham had lots of time to waste when he signed Erin's yearbook during D-Hall.

His signature started with an oversized "G" with "raham" written inside of it in smaller letters. Right next to it was an oversized "C" with "handler" written inside of it in smaller letters. He then finished by underlining his signature.

Other than his love of doodling, Graham wasn't sure why he had spent so much time perfecting his autograph. It came in handy, though, since he regularly signed dozens of them for kids after home basketball games, never failing to make him feel happy and at least a little bit like he played for the Spurs himself.

Erin then flipped to the next page, where Katy had signed her name and written her a note in black ink in the bottom right corner of the page:

> To my best friend Erin,
> You are the sweetest person I have ever met. I know we'll still be friends long after we get out of Trinity Springs High School. In fact, I fully expect us to go to college together. I'm thinking maybe the University of Texas. You could see yourself living in Austin, right? We would also both look damn good in burnt orange! Don't ever change who you are.
> Love ya lots and forever,
> Katy Christoval
> Class of '87
> Hook 'em Horns

Although Erin had glanced at the yearbook once or twice since Katy's death, it was the first time she had gone back and consecutively read what Katy and Graham had written.

She had completely forgotten the part about Katy saying they should go to school together at the University of Texas, where she had helped Trinity Springs win state in one-act play. It had never occurred to Erin both Graham and Katy had mentioned Austin when they signed her yearbook.

Like she had done several times before, Erin wondered what would have happened had she gone to Austin with Katy the day she died, if she could have maybe prevented the wreck from happening by being with her.

Or would she be dead, too? Seeing Katy mention Austin in her own handwriting sent a chill up and down her spine.

But there was also something strange about the two messages. Katy had signed her yearbook just a week or so before she died, and Erin hadn't gone to Austin with her go to shopping that day — even with the University of Texas and Austin so fresh on Katy's mind.

Erin went back and read Katy's message one more time. She thought: We could have spent some time driving around town, looking at campus and some possible places to live in between shopping if I had gone with her. We could have made a real day of it.

In fact, Katy hadn't even told Erin she was going to Austin the day she died … not a word about it. She found out where Katy had been that day when Graham called to tell her that her best friend was dead on the side of FM 38.

6

KYLE UTLEY

Kyle was more than a little surprised to see Graham sitting in the gym bleachers all by himself a couple of minutes after the final bell rang on the third day of school. They didn't have athletics on Wednesday afternoons during the first six weeks of the school year.

As he walked past the gymnasium after Civics, his final class of the day, Kyle caught a glimpse of Graham through his peripheral vision through the glass on the gym doors.

He stopped to take a better look inside. Kyle saw his best friend without Graham noticing him at all. Kyle had seen Graham a hundred times inside that gym, but the sight of him sitting alone in the empty stands was like seeing him in there for the first time. It just wasn't computing in his brain.

Kyle expected things might be weird for Graham early in the school year, but that didn't mean he was necessarily prepared for when it happened.

Graham, even from a distance, looked somewhat dazed. He was sitting completely still with his hands resting on the bleachers. Six rows up from the floor on the visitors' side, he was just staring out across the other side of the gym toward the purple home stands.

Before he opened the door to the gym, Kyle thought for a moment about the night Graham scored 28 points in a huge district home game late in the previous season. It was a one-point win that helped them seal the district championship. He hadn't missed a single shot that night — 14-for-14.

His teammates dubbed Graham "Money" for the rest of the season after that performance. Plus, there was a huge photo of Graham in the newspaper shooting the rock the next day. The picture was so perfectly framed it looked like it could have been on a trading card or something.

Katy got five copies of the paper that day, even though Graham's photo had previously been in the newspaper several times. This one was in color. And it was her favorite photo of him playing basketball.

Kyle had never seen Graham act quite like this before. Even in the aftermath of Katy's death, he mostly stayed home and kept to himself. For the first two days, he didn't even leave his house once — not even to go on an E-Z Mart run for snacks.

Kyle knew Graham had to deal with Katy's death and grieve in his own way, and that had him worried.

Slowly, Graham started to return to his normal self. But Kyle could tell that Katy never really left his thoughts — at least not for more than a few seconds — in the last three months. And he wondered what that must be like to endure.

Kyle gently pressed open one of the gym doors. The door made a squeaking sound and snapped Graham out of his daze. His eyes immediately darted toward Kyle.

Once they made eye contact, Graham quickly motioned for him to come over as the gym lights incessantly buzzed like a small colony of bees.

"Man, I sure am glad to see you right now," he said to Kyle from across the gymnasium, his voice echoing over the noise from the lights. "Come on up."

Kyle didn't reply. Instead, he just started walking down the baseline. He couldn't imagine what would cause Graham to sit all alone in an empty gym.

As he walked across the gym, Kyle looked out at the big Sidewinders logo in the middle of the floor, up at the 1983-84, 1984-85 and 1985-86 district championship banners and then back at Graham. Kyle gave him a knowing nod of approval and his own shit-eating grin.

Just like in practice, Kyle's sneakers squeaked as he walked across the floor, causing an even louder echo in the vacant and frigid gymnasium. Kyle continued to train his eyes on Graham as he started making his way up the bleachers.

"Chandler, what the hell are you doing sitting in here all by yourself? It's Wednesday, dude. We're Casper, bro."

There were at least 15 seconds of silence before Graham finally started to tell Kyle what was weighing so heavily on his mind.

"I've got some pretty fucked up shit to tell you about, man."

"Sure," Kyle said, straddling the bleacher sideways right in front of Graham. "Seriously, man, is everything cool?"

"I don't know. I honestly don't have the slightest idea how to answer that fucking question right now, Kyle."

With concern in his voice, Kyle answered, "What's wrong? Tell me what happened. It's me, Kyle, your brother from another mother."

Graham looked at Kyle for a few more seconds before finally mustering an answer. "Um, wow. Where should I start?"

There was yet another long pause by Graham as he took a few more seconds to gather his thoughts and explain.

"Um, I just got finished having a conversation with Tyler. We skipped sixth period and hung out in the back of the library so we could talk. You know, like Katy and Erin used to?"

"Holy shit. So, you asked him what he meant about helping you see Katy?"

"Yeah, I damn sure did. I was going to talk to him yesterday, but he bailed school early. ... Kyle, seriously, this shit is absolutely fucking crazy, man."

Graham took a deep breath and heavily let it out.

"So, we sit down in the library, which was pretty much completely empty. I figured it would be a nice, quiet place where I probably wouldn't raise my voice if I got upset again. I went into it with a pretty open mind, actually. I really wanted to hear what the dude had to say for himself."

"Uh-huh."

"We told the librarian we had to work on a project during class time. And it somehow worked. I guess she didn't think about the fact it was only the third day of school."

"Yeah," Kyle said, hanging on every word as he shifted and raised his voice in anticipation. "So, what happened? What did he say, Graham? Tell me."

"We start to make small talk for a little bit again — you know, about how he likes the school, what he thinks of everybody, why he left early Tuesday — all of that kind of shit. And then he says the same damn thing again: 'Graham, I'm not bullshitting you. I really can really help you see Katy again.'

"I started to get pissed off all over again, but then I counted to 10, stayed calm and asked him, 'What exactly do you mean by that, Tyler?'"

Graham paused for a few seconds as the gym lights continued to buzz. Kyle looked at him in bewilderment.

"He tells me that he can arrange it so I can see Katy for just one more day. 'I can absolutely make it happen, but only for 24 hours — no more, no less,' he says, cool as a fucking cucumber."

"What? Like some kind of time travel crap?" Kyle said, now in complete disbelief. "Come on, dude. What the hell is that shit all about?"

"I know, I know. It doesn't make one damn bit of sense. You know what, though, Kyle? The really weird thing is that I totally believed him, man. I asked him how in the hell that would be possible?

"He just told me that he couldn't say how he could do it — only that he could do it. He said, 'Graham, this is for real, man.' He was very insistent. And you know I can usually tell when somebody's yanking my chain, right?"

"Yeah, man. Always. Your bullshit detector is easily the best one I've ever run across. It almost goes off before somebody even opens their mouth to bullshit you. I should know."

"Kyle, I really, really believed him. I don't know why, but I just did — deep down in my gut. He said it with such conviction and supreme confidence in himself. He looked me right in the eyes every damn time he said it, too. It was like it was just a matter of fucking fact. Even though it isn't possible, he believes it is. He thinks he can honestly help me see Katy one more time."

"So, you said you would do it? Holy fucking shit, Graham!" Kyle said as his voice started to get louder and more intense. "This is completely insane."

"I told him I'd have to think about it. He said to take my time and let him know whenever I was ready. I wanted to make sure I thought it through and talked it over with you before I make a decision.

"He wrote down his number for me and told me to call him whenever I have an answer. Like I said before … supreme confidence in himself. It was like he already knew I was going to say yes. It was spooky."

Kyle sat and thought about the absolute bomb Graham had just dropped on him, trying to somehow come to terms with the possibility there might be a chance Tyler was completely on the up and up.

It was just so hard to believe. Especially coming from a guy who plays guitar in a band called Evening Wood.

"I really don't think you should do this, Graham. He might have sounded sincere, but I don't think you should get your hopes up, man. I think you're just setting yourself up for a letdown.

"You can't go back in time — especially with some guitar-playing, cool-looking new kid from Austin you've known for 72 hours as your fucking tour guide! It's not possible. And that's all there is to it."

"But what if it is possible, Kyle? How could I pass up that opportunity to tell Katy goodbye and see her one final time? Think about it, man. One more chance for me to see her face, to hold her, to kiss her, to tell her how beautiful she is, to tell her I love her. I don't think it's real at all, but what if it is?"

Kyle continued trying to let all of what Graham was telling him sink in, but the more he tried to make sense of it all, the more his head just continued to spin. He already knew Graham was going to tell Tyler he would do it. He could see it in his eyes.

"So, when would this happen? When would you see her? Would it be the day she, you know … died? Would it be just some random day? Would you be right back to the here and now, like the next day? Would it even be since we started high school? Would we even know you were gone?"

"I don't know the answers to any of those questions, man. All I know is he said he could make it happen. And I fucking believe him. I was completely skeptical before we sat down to talk.

"I guess if I had a choice, I would try to see her a day or two before she died so I could maybe warn her and maybe, you know, stop it from happening."

"Hold up just one damn second, Chandler. You can't be doing that shit! You remember what happened in *Back to the Future*, right? People will start disappearing from photos and shit because you altered the fucking future. You have to keep things the way they happened.

"What am I saying? Dude, this is ridiculous. I can't believe we're having this conversation. It just can't be real, period!"

"I know, but I have to leave open the possibility, Kyle," Graham answered with his voice starting to shake. "How could I not? I miss her so much, man. And if I could just at least tell her goodbye, I think it would be worth it.

"You know I never got to say goodbye to her, Kyle. I didn't even talk to her the day she died. I was surprised she didn't take Erin or her Mom or somebody with her to Austin for company. If it were you, you'd have to know what happened that day, wouldn't you?"

"Okay," Kyle finally relented. "Please just don't get too caught up in this. I don't know who the hell this guy is, or why in the hell he's telling you this stuff, but it's really kind of freaking me out."

"Freaking you out? I don't know if I even believe it's real. Hell, it's probably just wishful thinking, but I've got to know for sure. Otherwise, it will be in the back of my mind forever.

"I tried to get him to tell me more, but he wouldn't budge on any actual details other than it would be for 24 hours. I don't even know how he found out about what happened to Katy. He didn't say.

"Maybe somebody told him before school started. Maybe that's what makes me believe him … like he just knew about it, through osmosis or something like that. Crap, I don't know, Kyle."

The two sat silently on the bleachers together for a few more seconds.

"Okay," Kyle finally said. "Let's get the hell out of here. Christ, this is weirder than the time we messed with the Ouija Board in ninth grade and lights and televisions started turning themselves on and off and shit. Remember that?"

"Uh, yeah. How could I forget? It scared the crap out of all of us. I never thought I'd be in the middle of the woods, in the middle of the night, burning a freaking Ouija Board. Thank God Erin finally talked some sense into us."

As they finally stood up and started walking down the stands toward the basketball court to head home, Coach Elgin emerged from his office after hearing some conversation going on.

"Coach E!" Kyle yelled. "What's up?"

"Utley, Chandler. You two just feel like spending your afternoon off in the gym, huh? I like your enthusiasm, ladies. We're still a little ways off from the season starting, but you're always welcome to practice on your own as much as you want.

"It damn sure wouldn't hurt either one of you to shoot some free throws. I think you were both at like, what, 75 percent last year? We could get that up to 80 with some hard work. Do you want me to get you a couple of basketballs out for you?"

"No, coach, we were just shooting the bull," Graham said, "and leaving."

"If you practiced as much as you chatted, we might have a better shot at getting past the Regional finals this year," he barked.

"Oh, it's going to happen this time," Kyle said. "We're going to Austin and winning state, damn it. You can go ahead and write that down and book the hotel rooms, Coach E."

"Damn right," Graham echoed, slapping Kyle five.

"Once again, I like the enthusiasm," he answered, giving a small wave to them as he headed back to his office.

Kyle and Graham walked outside and back to their cars, which were parked two spaces apart in the nearly empty senior parking lot. Kyle got into his car and watched as Graham pulled away.

As he left the parking lot, Graham gave his horn a couple of short honks. In all fairness, it totally sounded like it was circa World War II.

Kyle sat still for a couple of minutes in his car thinking about what Graham had just told him. As much as he hated to admit it, Kyle was just as curious about what Tyler had said as Graham. If Tyler had been somebody they had known for a long time telling Graham he could help him see Katy, it would have been a lot easier to completely pass it all off as crap.

The fact Tyler was pretty much a stranger only seemed to add more intrigue to his outrageous claim. Plus, he was so adamant about it even after the blowup in the cafeteria. The whole situation was starting to seem like something out of some really creepy movie, Kyle thought.

Kyle also couldn't help but think about how he would handle it if he were in Graham's shoes. Would he have just started wailing on Tyler in the cafeteria? Probably. But if Tyler wasn't bullshitting, what would he do if he had the chance to see his dead girlfriend again who he never got to tell goodbye?

Sure, he'd tell her that he loved her and everything, but could he even handle seeing her again and not telling her that she was going to die? And before she even saw her senior year of high school?

There's no way he could possibly know that, but he figured it could lead to some pretty disastrous results. He also thought seeing Katy again might do a lot more harm than good to Graham.

And could Graham really stop Katy from being killed if he tried? He was legitimately worried about where the situation was headed.

"Man, I don't like this," he sighed before finally turning the key in the ignition to start his car.

The sun was still blazing in the afternoon sky. Kyle thought he would stop by the cemetery to see Katy's grave before he went home. He continued to think about the possible circumstances of a visit between people from different planes of existence.

"This is so messed up," Kyle said.

Kyle started to drive to Longview Cemetery. As he did, he turned on the radio just in time to hear some Dead or Alive. He cranked the volume as high as it would go as he drove off.

"These go to 11," he said, doing his best Nigel Tufnell impression during a short break from his off-key and extremely loud sing-a-long with "Lover Come Back to Me."

On the way, Kyle thought about Graham saying he hadn't even seen Katy the day she died. That wasn't the case for Kyle.

In fact, he was the only one of Katy's friends that did see her that fateful day. That chance encounter happened a little after 8:45 a.m., inside the E-Z Mart. Kyle stopped in to grab a quick bite before he left for his part-time job bagging groceries at H-E-B.

When he walked into the convenience store, the chime went off to alert the clerk somebody was coming through the front door, prompting Katy to look over from where she was, standing near the drink coolers.

Katy was wearing a Phoenix Hard Rock Café T-shirt and blue jeans. She was holding a bottle of Dr Pepper she had just grabbed from the cooler.

When she spotted Kyle, she gave him a cursory wave and smile. He waved and smiled back before making his way to the snack cakes aisle for some doughnuts, and then to the coolers to grab a carton of milk.

Katy simultaneously made her way to the register to pay for her drink and a pack of grape Bubble Yum.

Since he was distracted by getting his breakfast and was in a bit of a hurry, Kyle hadn't even noticed Katy walk out the door, but he heard the chime go off again as she did.

Once she left, Kyle and the clerk were the only two people left in the E-Z Mart. By the time he paid for his food and drink, Katy had already driven off in her mom's car, which Victoria let her borrow on occasion.

Kyle didn't think anything about the fact he and Katy hadn't actually spoken to one another at the time, but he damn sure thought about it plenty of times after she was gone. In fact, Kyle practically strained his brain trying to remember every mundane detail about her during those 55 seconds or so.

The more he thought about it, he did find it a little bit weird that they hadn't said a single word to one another. He tried to remember the last time they had been in such close proximity without at least saying "hello" and having a brief conversation since they had become friends.

And she was just going to Austin to shop. She couldn't have been in any kind of a hurry, he remembered thinking. It was so early in the morning. The stores probably weren't even going to be open when she got there. Why didn't she wait for me to come outside to at least say hi?

He had asked that question and gone over his encounter with Katy at least three or four times with Graham. He had told Graham almost everything about it.

The lack of conversation between them was odd, but it wasn't like they walked right past one another or anything — they were on opposite sides of the store.

The one thing Kyle never divulged to anybody about that day was there was something just a tad bit different about Katy. He wasn't sure he could even put his finger on what exactly it was that seemed different, which was exactly the reason he never said a word.

Had she done her hair a little differently? Was she wearing something Kyle had never seen her wear before? Or was it just some sort of weird premonition he had about what was coming later that evening? Something was just off a little bit. Even in that incredibly short amount of time, he could sense it.

Kyle was convinced it would have done a lot more harm than good if he had said anything to anybody. So, he never told a soul, but it was the only thing he could think about on the short ride to Longview Cemetery.

Once he arrived, Kyle parked his car, got out and walked over to Katy's grave, breaking a little bit of a sweat. He stood over the plot of land and stared at her tombstone and the wilted yellow roses leaning up against it.

"This Tyler guy is completely full of shit," Kyle said.

After standing there in silence for a couple of minutes and looking at Katy's gravestone, he told Katy goodbye and got back into his car.

As he started to drive off, Kyle knew there was no way he could go straight home and spend the rest of the night thinking about everything on his mind. He had to talk to somebody other than Graham to hear another point of view.

As he came up to the next crossroad, Kyle turned right onto it and turned around in the other direction.

"This is so fucked up," he said. A few drops of rain started to fall out of the sky, even though it was still at least 92 degrees.

As the rain started to hit his windshield, in his best Cockney accent, Kyle said, "The *rain* in *Spain* falls mainly on the *plain*."

7

ABBOTT ELGIN

Graham and Kyle had been gone from the gymnasium for around an hour. Abbott was camped out at his desk reading the newspaper when he heard a familiar, gentle knock on his office door.

He smiled and looked down at his watch with the paper still outstretched in his hands before promptly bolting out of his chair.

"Right on time," he said loud enough for the person on the other side of the door to hear him. He folded the newspaper, dropped it on his desk, and then excitedly walked over toward the door.

When he opened the door, there stood Elsa Hitchcock, briefcase in hand and a beautiful smile on her face. A waft of her perfume, Christian Dior's Poison, which she had sprayed on about five minutes earlier, quickly found its way to his nose. He gave her a smile back as they locked eyes for the first time in a couple of weeks.

"Hello there, Vertigo."

"Hello there, Coach Hard-Ass," Elsa replied, as she walked through the door, closing it behind her using her right foot, and not taking her eyes off of him.

Once she was in the office and the door was shut, she immediately dropped her briefcase to the ground. She reached out and firmly embraced Abbott, who grabbed her around her waist and gently squeezed her. The two of them engaged in a long, passionate kiss.

Both Elsa and Abbott were married, but they had been having an affair for several months. It all started when their marriages were struggling right after the holidays, with school — and district play in basketball — starting again. Neither one of them had ever cheated on their spouses.

They were just about the same age. Both of them had always found the other to be the most attractive teacher of the opposite sex at Trinity Springs High School, although Melissa Campbell and Heath Denton at least prevented those two races from being complete landslides.

Abbott and Elsa had exchanged glances at staff meetings and basketball games long before anything ever developed between the two of them.

One day after basketball practice, Abbott noticed Elsa's car was still in the teachers' parking lot, so he wandered over to her classroom to see if she happened to still be around.

She was sitting at her desk grading papers and less than five minutes from packing up and leaving for the day.

He knocked on her classroom door, ducked his head inside and asked, "Do you want to go get a cup of coffee or grab a bite to eat some time?" Even by his standards, it was a pretty damn ballsy move.

"No, thank you. I am a married woman, Coach Elgin," she answered, pretty much nipping any ideas of screwing around with her he might have had right in the bud. Still, she was extremely flattered and more than a little turned on by the attention from another man she found so attractive.

It was only two days later, after she had pretty much constantly thought about Abbott's invitation, she showed up at his office door one afternoon not long after basketball practice.

Because Abbott's assistant coaches, Ross Sealy and Lucas Timpson, were still there that day, Elsa said she had to speak with him about one of his player's performance in the classroom. That was how it all started, although they weren't able to really see each other and talk in private until two or three days later.

The two of them hit it off immediately and agreed they would have a fling that would be just for fun — no strings attached. Nobody gets hurt, they had agreed from the get-go.

Ironically, both of their marriages seemed to get somewhat back on course about two months later. Maybe Abbott and Elsa having sex with somebody other than their spouses somehow helped them see things in a little bit different light and right their matrimonial ships, so to speak. At least that's the way Abbott saw it.

The hardest part of their affair was the sneaking around — especially in such a small town. They couldn't possibly do much of anything together in Trinity Springs or they would be spotted for sure.

Even so much as riding in a car together carried pretty significant risk. So, they were pretty much limited to late-afternoon rendezvous in either his office or her classroom, when they were typically the only two people remaining at school. Actually, the only *three* people remaining at the school — them and the custodian vigorously vacuuming the carpet in those long-ass hallways.

The gym was much more preferable, seeing as how it was somewhat secluded from the rest of the school and significantly more private than her classroom.

Plus, Abbott parked his pickup truck right outside of the gym, so it wasn't completely obvious at a glance to anybody who might be driving by the front of the school that their cars were almost the only ones left in the parking lot.

If anybody ever found out, they'd be fired on the spot for sure. School boards tend to look down on married teachers banging each other on school grounds, after all. Or any teachers banging each other on school grounds, for that matter.

Two or three times, they found a way to meet in Austin or San Antonio late on a Saturday or Sunday afternoon. But, even then they had to do tons of strategic planning and reconnaissance and be extremely careful because so many people from Trinity Springs also went to those cities on weekends on a regular basis.

No matter how much they planned things out, they could easily bump into a student, the parents of a student or another basketball coach Abbott knew. Their spouses both seemed pretty oblivious to what was going on, never raising an eyebrow of suspicion. That helped make the guilt Abbott and Elsa felt go down just a little bit easier.

They just saw each other when they could, enjoyed each other's company and tried not to pay too much attention to the wedding bands on the second finger of their left hands. They had both become pretty good at ignoring those rings.

The danger factor also seemed to make things more exciting and fun. They both felt like they were still in high school sometimes — the jock and the brain, getting it on like rabbits while trying to keep their affair a secret.

Of course, things were even more intense between them with school starting again. They had only managed to see each other three times over the course of the entire summer, and they hadn't even laid eyes on one another on the first two days of classes with all of the hustle and bustle going on.

One time when Abbott's wife, Anna, was out of town for the weekend, they were able to see each other two straight nights in town. Elsa told her husband, Kirby, she had to go to a two-day conference in Corpus Christi, which was a pretty damn ballsy move itself.

They sat together on the living room couch at Abbott's place eating pizza and talking the first night. Elsa parked her car in Abbott's garage so there would be no danger of anybody spotting it. He went and picked up the pizza and Lone Star Beer by himself.

The second night, they took a late-night drive out to the lake and went on a midnight boat ride underneath the stars. Both nights were truly among the best times Elsa ever had in her life.

Whenever they were together, Abbott treated her like a queen, which was really the only way he had ever treated all of the women in his life — outside of cheating on his wife, of course.

The fact their relationship was so casual also made it easy to be themselves around each other, which they were both still struggling to do around their spouses at times.

Elsa's husband had reached the point in their marriage where he mostly wanted to come home from work, watch TV, and then go to straight to sleep with no notions of romance.

Elsa even suspected maybe he was getting some on the side, too. He didn't really seem the type to fool around, but then again neither did she. Or Abbott. She thought how ironic it would be if their spouses also happened to be screwing around on them with one another.

"You're going to have to take me out of town sometime soon," Elsa said, still embracing Abbott. "Maybe we could go somewhere other than Austin or San Antonio, like Las Vegas or somewhere else really fun and romantic."

"Oh, yeah? Why is that?"

"I want to go on a real date with you, Abbott. We need to go to a movie or something — you know, like a couple. We need to make out in the back of the theater. I want us to be able to go out and not have to be constantly worried about getting caught."

"Elsa, you know damn well there's no way in the world we can do that."

"Why not?"

"What in the hell would we tell our spouses?" Abbott said, his voice slightly starting to increase in volume like he was barking at one of his players while conducting a three-man weave. "Hey, honey, I'm going to Vegas this weekend. Is that cool?

"We'd be so incredibly screwed if we got caught. Our marriages would end. We'd lose our jobs. Then we couldn't even afford to go to a movie. Do you want to stand in an unemployment line with me? That would be awfully damn fun and romantic, wouldn't it?"

Elsa couldn't argue with his logic, so she just embraced the moment for what it was. She was well aware she was fighting a losing battle.

"You're right, Abbott," she said. "Can you imagine how creeped out our students would be if they ever found out about us?"

Both of them erupted in laughter. It was certainly a subject they had broached before, but the very thought of some of their students picturing "Vertigo" and "Coach Hard-Ass" getting it on in his office, or her classroom, after school was always good for a hearty chuckle.

"I would probably go up a notch or two in my players' books. They'd think it was radical or bitchin' or some stupid shit like that."

"I don't think my students would think it was radical or bitchin'. Hell, they'd probably wonder if I gave you a homework assignment or a pop quiz after we were finished."

Both of them laughed again. They shared another passionate kiss, as Abbott slowly slid his hands down and grabbed Elsa's ass, just like he had done at least a dozen or so times before in that very spot. Abbott had, appropriately, always been an ass man.

Early on in their fling, they came pretty close to getting caught. It was a good 90 minutes after basketball practice was over one Wednesday in February. Coach Timpson and Coach Sealy had already gone home when Abbott and Elsa were half naked in his office.

Suddenly, they heard the locker room door open behind them, a mere few feet outside of Abbott's office. It was Vernon Wylie. Had Abbott's office door been open, they would have been absolutely busted, dead to right, standing there in their underwear in front of a student.

"Holy shit!" Abbott said in a whisper. "Quick, Elsa, you've got to hide, baby. Hurry!"

As she made her way to the small bathroom connected to his office, Abbott quickly got dressed and scurried into the locker room, tucking his T-shirt into his shorts as he hustled out of the door as quickly as he could.

Elsa could barely hear Abbott talk to the best player he had ever coached from her spot in the bathroom. She thought about how Abbott could smooth over practically any situation. She tried her best to hear their conversation and prayed to God their cover hadn't been blown.

"Vernon," Coach Elgin said, trying his damndest to have an ordinary tone of voice. "What are you doing back here, son? Didn't get enough practice? You can always work on your free-throw shooting. Do you want me to get you a ball?"

"Oh, no. I forgot my Walkman, coach. I can't live without my tunes, you know? I got all the way home and had to come back. What are you still doing here?"

"Um, I'm just doing some extra scouting. You know, getting a little extra film in for the playoffs — that's all. You never can be too prepared for the postseason, right?"

"Cool, cool. Man, you're a workaholic, coach. But that's why you're the best in the business, right?"

"Damn straight. Of course, having a player like you makes my job a hell of a lot easier. Have a good one, Vernon. Get some rest tonight. You're going to need it for practice tomorrow. We've got a big one on the road against Dupree on Friday night."

"You know it, Coach E."

Vernon strolled out of the locker room and back to his car in one of the senior parking spaces, his Walkman blaring his favorite tape, LL Cool J's *Radio*.

When he got into his car, he looked back toward the gym. Something almost made him get back out and make sure Coach Elgin was really being straight with him … just an odd feeling he had, more than anything else.

Instead, he transferred the tape he was listening to from his Walkman to his car stereo and drove off without even noticing Mrs. Hitchcock's car sitting by itself in the front parking lot. The bass in his speakers started to boom, and he started rapping along to "Dear Yvette."

The trickiest part of the affair had always been keeping it a secret from his two assistant coaches, although they usually left school before Abbott. He and Elsa never imagined they'd have to try to keep it from one of his players once practice was long over.

Abbott had always been extremely detail-oriented, so if his assistants had some reason to stay late on a day he and Elsa planned to meet, he always found an excuse to get them out of there earlier than they had planned. He usually made it seem to them like it was their idea to leave early, too.

Abbott was able to apply his skills just as effectively to getting some on the side as he was to making a game plan for his team before a huge game.

When he married Anna, Abbott had been in on the wedding planning just as much as she had, which wasn't exactly the norm for a hard-assed high school basketball coach. But he wanted to make sure every detail for the big day was just right, which made perfect sense given his propensity for attention to detail.

They got married on a beautiful sunny afternoon in Palestine, in East Texas, where Anna grew up, six years earlier. Abbott still loved Anna very much, but there was just something exciting about Elsa that fueled his ego and made him feel completely alive. Plus, she was just so hot and smelled so damn good.

But, Abbott wouldn't have intentionally hurt Anna for all of the money in the world. Overall, they were still reasonably happy together, so Abbott pretty much just figured he'd have his cake and eat it, too, for as long as he could. He figured Elsa would eventually get fed up with the arrangement and that would be that.

Finally, Abbott and Elsa let go of one another and sat down. Ever the basketball coach, Abbott started the conversation back up with, "So, what about this new kid? Nixon, is it? Does he look like he can play basketball or what?"

"Um, no," Elsa quickly replied, rolling her eyes a bit and holding back a little laughter at the thought. "He looks like the type you'd be hard pressed to get to even sit still for a couple of hours to watch a basketball game. He looks like he's into rock and roll, not jump shots."

"Hmm, that sucks. Although I do believe we'll be just fine without any extra help this year, you can never have too much depth.

"Elsa, this is absolutely going to be the best team I've ever coached — no doubt about it in my mind. If we can stay away from injuries, we have a pretty legitimate shot to go undefeated. Damn, that would be incredible. Hell, we only lost three times last year."

"I heard Tyler talking to Graham Chandler after class the other day, though. It sounded like he had said something to really upset Graham the day before. That struck me as pretty odd considering it was Tyler's first day here and the first day of school. It sounded like Graham had calmed down about whatever happened, and all was well in class this morning. Is Graham going to cause trouble and be a pain in my ass, Abbott?"

"God, no," he answered emphatically. "Graham's a great kid. He's been through a hell of a lot, you know? Seeing him at Katy's funeral just about broke my heart.

"Losing your girlfriend in high school has got to be pretty damn devastating. Dealing with something like that at any age is tough, but it's hard for me to imagine dealing with it while you're still in freaking high school.

"Everything is such a big deal when you're in high school, Elsa. You know that just as well as I do. I have been really worried about Graham since Katy died.

"That's one tough kid to go through what he's gone through and still be the same, grounded person he's always been. And he doesn't need some damn outsider coming in here and messing with brain and getting him all screwed up — especially with basketball season coming up in a couple of months."

"You're absolutely right. Everything is so much bigger of a deal when you're that young. Some people never get over that kind of thing, you know? At least he seems to have some good friends around him to help him cope with it all."

"I hope he can stay on track. That kid could play basketball in college. He might not go to some massive school, but he could be a hell of a player for a smaller school — maybe a junior college, like Kilgore or Trinity Valley. I'll do my best to keep an eye on him. You do the same, huh?"

"I will. I promise I'll keep my eye on Tyler, too."

"Sounds good, Vertigo."

Elsa stood up and gently slapped Abbott across the face.

"You watch your mouth, Coach Hard Ass."

"Elsa, you know I like it rough."

The two embraced again, slowly removing each other's clothes. Abbott locked eyes with Elsa and gave her his own shit-eating grin as he removed her purple panties.

As they started to make love on his desk, she couldn't help but think about her favorite Shakespeare sonnet. She started to recite it in her mind, changing the last line to *she* thinks no ill, as usual.

Elsa knew there wasn't a chance in hell she could tell Abbott how head-over-heels in love she was with him. And, deep down, she knew there really wasn't any kind of future for them.

She knew she really didn't amount to anything more than just a side thing for Abbott, and she told herself from the beginning that's all it had to be for her. That was what she had agreed to, after all.

But Abbott was unlike any guy she had ever known. He was smart, funny and great at his job — all things that had always met her standards for a soul mate.

He also just knew how to talk to her, how to say the right things at the right times, which isn't easy to do when you're seeing an English teacher. Plus, the sex was amazing, which another strong selling point.

As Abbott continued to make passionate love to her, his mind began to drift off to the looming basketball season and what it would feel like to win his first state championship. After all, you don't get the nickname "Coach Hard-Ass" for nothing.

8

VERNON WYLIE

Vernon was in his driveway practicing free throws as the bright orange sun was setting in the clear Texas sky. He had literally shot thousands of free throws in his driveway, and his dedication had paid off in a big way.

Vernon had already committed to play basketball at the University of Texas at El Paso, which was really a pretty huge deal considering he played for such a small Class 3A high school.

Very few basketball players from Trinity Springs had ever even gone on to play college hoops at any level — especially before Coach Elgin arrived to lead the Sidewinders. And the few players who did move on to play college basketball did so for much smaller programs than UTEP.

Vernon was just that damn good.

He was big, athletic and smooth as a baby's bottom. There was practically nothing he couldn't do with a basketball. Vernon was a great shooter from just about any spot on the court, could defend the hell out of anybody and was an absolute rebounding machine.

Back in junior high, Vernon was six inches taller than any of his teammates. And before he moved on to Trinity Springs High School, he was already dunking the ball on the regulation goals with ease. Most of his teammates had to settle for dunking on the eight-foot goals near the junior high school playground.

Coach Elgin practically had to change his shorts he was so excited for Vernon to finally get to high school. Naturally, Vernon started on the varsity his freshman season. He was anything but some wide-eyed ninth-grader who looked overwhelmed.

In fact, Vernon averaged 15 points and 11 rebounds per game, easily helping him earn the district's newcomer of the year award at the end of that season.

Vernon was actually upset he wasn't the MVP, but he took home that honor his sophomore and junior seasons. He was also First-Team All-State his junior year, which was not much consolation for just missing a trip to the state tourney.

Nobody, including Coach Elgin, took it harder than Vernon when Trinity Springs lost to Prescott in the Regional finals. He finished with 31 points, 15 rebounds and five blocks, but he still somehow felt like he could have done more to help his team.

Vernon sulked around for more than two weeks after that game — especially after Prescott went on to win the whole damn thing. Vernon was absolutely determined not to let a loss in the Regional final happen again. He knew his team had the talent to go all the way.

This time, they were going to beat Prescott. This time, they were going to be the ones to win the state championship and hoist that damn trophy up in the air for the world to see.

When he closed his eyes, Vernon could envision it all happening in his mind's eye. And the vision of winning a title never failed to bring a smile to his face.

"Fuck Prescott!" he said as he drained yet another 20-footer. "We're going to whip some Bulldog behind this year, damn it."

Vernon reached down to get a drink of water from the plastic cup he had sitting on the edge of the concrete when he heard a car pull up behind him.

He quickly looked back over his shoulder to see it was Kyle and Kermit. He wasn't expecting any company, but those guys were pretty much family, so he wasn't at all surprised to see them.

Of course, they were always welcome at his house. Hell, hardly a day or two ever went by when three of the four friends didn't show up unannounced at one of the other one's house just to goof around, play video games or shoot some hoops. They were pretty inseparable, on and off the court.

"What's up, fellas?" Vernon said before taking another massive gulp of water and wiping the puddle of sweat from his brow with the sleeve of his shirt. "Man, it's hotter than a microwave out here."

"Do you ever do anything but play basketball?" Kermit asked.

"Nope. And that's why I abuse you in practice like a bitch every damn day."

"Ha ha, very funny. I will whip your black ass in H-O-R-S-E or 21 any damn day of the week, bitch."

"Guys, guys!" Kyle interrupted. "We're not here for any of that shit right now. Are we, Kermit?"

"No, man," Kermit replied in a more serious, rational tone of voice. "I'm sorry. Kyle's absolutely right. Dude, we've really got to talk to you about some pretty serious shit."

"All right, bet. Let's all go inside the house. We can go talk in my bedroom. This must be about some damn chick." That comment caused Kermit and Kyle to make eye contact.

After passing through the house and exchanging hellos and hugs with Vernon's sisters and mother, Kyle and Kermit each grabbed drinks of their own from the fridge. Kyle even managed to sneak a couple of chocolate chip cookies from the cookie jar when nobody was looking.

The air conditioning was working some serious overtime, and the television was blaring as the teammates and good friends made their way through the house.

Once they arrived to the serenity of Vernon's room, Kermit and Kyle both grabbed a chair as Vernon blotted off with a towel before plopping down in his favorite chair, right underneath his George Gervin "Iceman" poster. Like he had rehearsed it, Vernon was sitting in almost an identical pose to Gervin.

Vernon's room was essentially a shrine to basketball. His shelves were filled with his trophies, ribbons, pictures of teams he played on and books about the history of basketball and the NBA. The walls were covered in posters of his favorite players — Moses Malone and Dominique Wilkins, among others. Of course, he also had a Spurs pennant.

But the Gervin poster had always been his favorite since Iceman was his all-time favorite player.

That poster of him sitting on blocks of ice with silver basketballs was just about the coolest thing Vernon had ever seen. He even wore No. 44 in Gervin's honor. Vernon could remember his dad taking him to see the Iceman play back when he was a kid first starting to love basketball.

"Dad, No. 44 for the Spurs is really good," he told his Dad the first time they went to a game at HemisFair Arena.

"Damn right, son," his Dad replied, giving him a pat on his head.

"So, what's on y'alls' so-called minds?" Vernon asked, fully leaning back into his chair, taking a sip of his Sprite. "Talk to me, fellas."

"It's Graham," Kyle said. "We're really worried about him. This new kid, Tyler, told him he could help him see Katy again, man."

"Say what?" Vernon asked as a quizzical look came across his face and he leaned forward in his chair. "See Katy again? What the hell does that shit mean?"

"That's exactly what I said," Kyle replied. "But the thing is I think Graham actually believes him. And I'm pretty sure he's going to go through with it … whatever the hell *it* is.

"I think it might really mess him up to get his hopes up for nothing. I'm not sure he can handle that kind of a major letdown, you know? It's only been three months since she died."

Vernon shot a look of concern at Kyle as he continued explaining to him what had happened.

"Graham talked to the new kid earlier today at school. They skipped class and went to the library. Graham said he didn't think the guy was bullshitting him at all. Before that, Graham didn't believe a single word of it. He was just pissed. That's what got me so freaked out."

"Yeah, man," Kermit said. "And you know Graham. If he's buying into what you're selling him, then you are, at the very least, coming off as being on the up and up. And doing so pretty fucking convincingly. Graham thinking this dude is telling him the truth might not turn out so well.

"I mean, Graham's a level-headed guy, but anybody could be messed up over some shit like that. That was his girl, man. That's why he was yelling at this spikey-haired motherfucker in the cafeteria on Monday at lunch."

"That's exactly right," Kyle said. "I saw Graham right after it happened. As I was coming back from lunch at McDonald's, he was pulling out of the parking lot, looking as pissed off as I've ever seen him before. His face was bright red. He was ready to kick Tyler's ass after he just met the dude."

Ever the voice of reason — on and off the court — Vernon let everything they had said sink in, took another swig of Sprite, and then finally offered up his opinion.

"I really think you guys are freaking out a little bit too much over this situation. Look, Graham can damn sure handle himself. You've seen it on the basketball court a hundred times. The dude almost never gets rattled by anything. He's got ice water in those white boy veins.

"He handled losing Katy better than any of us could have, right? And when this Tyler dude doesn't follow through on what he said, then that will be the end of it. His ass won't be telling Graham he can help him see a god damn thing after that, or he'll have to deal with all four of us."

Both Kyle and Kermit had the same look of reassurance on their faces after hearing what Vernon had to say about the situation.

"Yeah, I guess maybe you're right," Kyle said. "I just wish he wouldn't get his damn hopes up so much. If you would have heard how he was talking to me about it, you wouldn't have even believed it was Graham.

"I found him sitting all by himself in the bleachers of the gym after sixth period. He told me about how Tyler looked him in the eyes while he kept insisting over and over again he could help him see Katy. Just hearing something like that would screw with anybody's head … even Graham's."

"That girl had a damn lead foot," Vernon said. "She was sweet as she could be, but she drove faster than most dudes I know. That's so damn messed up that she's gone. But Graham's going to be cool — he's a warrior. Y'all just chill out, man.

"Hell, Graham probably doesn't even really believe it himself, deep down. He's probably just calling dude's bluff. Don't sweat it, y'all. By the end of the week, this whole thing will be straight up in the rearview."

With that, Kyle and Kermit seemed to feel much better than they had a few minutes earlier. But they were both still plenty concerned about what was going to happen with Graham, regardless of whether or not Tyler was telling the truth.

Vernon had at least helped them cope with the situation better. After sitting around talking about the new school year and the upcoming basketball season for a few more minutes, Kyle and Kermit were ready to leave.

"Thanks so much, bro," Kyle said as he hugged Vernon.

"That's what I'm here for. I don't know what the hell y'all are going to do after we graduate. Come out to El Paso for advice, I guess."

Vernon stood in his driveway and watched as they drove away. He thought about the conversation they had just had. He went back inside, picked up his car keys and told his Mom he'd be back in about 30 minutes.

"Make sure you're here in time for dinner, son," Charlotte Wylie answered. "We're having cubed steak, mashed potatoes and cream corn tonight. And it's your turn to set the …"

Vernon was already out the door as his Mom was finishing talking to him.

"...table."

A few miles away at his house, Graham's mind was going in a million different directions. He had just spoken to Tyler on the phone and told him that, after talking to Kyle about it, he definitely wanted his help. He wanted to see Katy again and tell her goodbye.

Graham figured once he said that he would do it, Tyler would surely fill him in with some more details about how exactly how it would all go down. But that wasn't the case at all. Tyler remained ambiguous about how the reunion with Katy would happen, sparing pretty much every detail.

"Okay, Graham," he said. "You will see Katy one more time."

Graham still didn't know when it would happen, or even what year it would be when he saw her again. Would it be the day she died? Hell, would it be five years ago? Would it be in fifth grade, when she moved to town and they first met?

When he asked Tyler those questions, he just said all he could tell Graham is that he would "see her soon." Finally, he said, "Later," and hung up the phone. Graham held the phone to his ear until he heard a dial tone. He was stunned.

Even though he wasn't happy about Tyler hanging up so abruptly, Graham once again got the overwhelming feeling the new kid was not yanking his chain — not even a little bit. He could feel it in his bones.

That's why Graham was really starting to get nervous. He thought about what exactly he would say to Katy, assuming any of this was real, and was replaying the short conversation he just had with Tyler in his head when he heard a car pull up in front of his house.

Before he heard the car, Graham was considering going over to Tyler's house and telling him to just forget all about the whole thing — that he changed his mind. But Graham realized that he didn't even know where the new kid lived, so he couldn't go to his house and talk to him in person. He only had the phone number Tyler had given to him after their conversation in the library.

Graham had already tried calling Tyler back twice, but each time the phone just rang about 10 times — never even going to an answering machine. Graham was now basically at Tyler's mercy, which was driving him all kinds of crazy.

Who in the hell is here?

Graham thought maybe it was Tyler coming over to fill him in with more details, for a moment forgetting Tyler didn't know where he lived. And that he didn't even know for sure if he had a car.

Instead, he saw Vernon's familiar 1983 blue Trans Am coming to a rest in the driveway.

"Shit," Graham said, almost in panic mode, scrambling toward the door. Graham opened the door just before Vernon could knock.

"What's up, my man?" Vernon asked, reaching his hand out to slap Graham five.

"What's up, dude?" he answered, instead grabbing Vernon's hand and shaking it.

"Can I come in, bro?"

"Of course you can, man. Mom's not home yet, so it's just us here. What's happening?"

"Look, man, the fellas told me about what went down with Tyler today. I thought I'd come over here and tell you I really don't think you should get too upset about it. You need to just ride the thing out and see what happens. Odds are this dude is bullshitting you. But, I agree with you, man, why not find out for sure?

"If you don't, it's just going to bother you for the rest of our senior year, and maybe the rest of your life. You can't just walk around with some bullshit like that hanging over your head, right?"

An eerie calm settled over Graham. Maybe it was just because he was hearing somebody else's opinion that made it seem more like everything was going to be okay. Or maybe it was simply that Vernon had a way of calmly putting things in perspective.

As upset as Vernon had been after the Prescott loss in the Regional finals, he was still the one who was going around the locker room comforting his teammates after the game.

Graham was sitting in front of his locker with a dazed look on his face when Vernon came up to him and said, "This sucks ass, but we've got another shot at it, Chandler. We ain't done yet. We're going to get it done. I know we are. Remember how this shit feels, man. Don't you ever forget it — just get stronger because of it." Graham recalled that conversation as he found Vernon once again reassuring him.

"Yeah, man. I just talked to Tyler a few minutes ago on the phone. I told him I wanted to do it, and then I asked him when it would happen and where I would see her? He didn't budge on one single detail. I was just kind of freaking out because I still don't know when this shit is supposed to go down.

"I assumed he would tell me exactly when I would see her again once I agreed to do it. I don't know … maybe he still has to figure that part out and get it all set up? I'll have to catch him after English class tomorrow morning, I guess."

"Yeah, dude," Vernon said as he tried to hide his complete disbelief of the idea Graham could ever possibly see his dead girlfriend again in this or any lifetime. "That must be what it is. Dude is just getting it all set up, that's all. We'll talk to this cat tomorrow at school and ask him what the deal is.

"Personally, I think he's going to have to come clean with you that he's full of shit. Maybe he's trying to be cute. Maybe that's the kind of dude he is — some kind of jokester or something like that.

"If that's the case, he won't be playing any more jokes any time soon. We'll see what's up with it, Chandler. We've always got your back, man."

Graham smiled and then reached out grabbed Vernon's hand to shake it.

"Man, I can't thank you enough for that. Dude, I was really flipping out since I decided to do it. I can't stop thinking about it. I just can't pass up the opportunity if it's really there. I have to see her again, tell her I love her."

"I don't blame you, man. It's going to be all right, Chandler. Everything's going to be fine. We're going to get this crap out of the way, whip Prescott's ass, win state and party our asses off the rest of our senior year. And then you are going to take a long-ass road trip to El Paso to watch me kick ass at UTEP, you dig?"

"Hell, yes, we're winning state," Graham said. "And I'm damn sure coming to El Paso to see you play."

"Austin is calling our damn names, son. Can you hear it?"

9

MELISSA HENDERSON

The stage lights went down, and the massive curtains shut with great gusto as the crowd erupted into applause. The Trinity Springs High School production of *Pygmalion* had just finished its performance, knocking it out of the park at the University Interscholastic League's Class 3A State One-Act Play Contest at the University of Texas in Austin.

Melissa Henderson couldn't help but grin in approval. The applause that echoed loudly in the auditorium was pure music to her ears. She closed her eyes to relish the moment she hoped would never end.

"Thank you, God," she whispered. "Thank you, thank you, thank you, God."

There was no doubt in her mind her cast had just put together its best possible performance at the best possible time. Trinity Springs was the last school to perform, which Melissa believed was the perfect slot at any competition. She couldn't believe not one single member of the cast and crew failed to achieve perfection over the last 45 minutes.

She had told her kids backstage before the contest started, "No matter what you do in that final spot, you will be fresh on the judges' minds when they convene to make their final decisions. If you kick butt, you are going to have a real shot at bringing this thing home." She paused momentarily to look at the faces and read the body language of her kids as they hung on her every word. "And I know you are going to kick butt and bring this thing home!"

The cast she had so painstakingly put together for weeks, just like she had done every year, erupted in a mixture of cheers and screams before going into the auditorium with their matching state T-shirts to watch the first two schools perform.

This was easily Melissa's best cast ever, and she had known it pretty much since the first full rehearsal. When their first run-through was over and the kids had all cleared out and headed home, she went into her office, shut the door and laughed, then cried tears of joy at the possibilities that lie ahead.

Melissa could feel ultimate victory — a feeling she had yearned for almost all of her life. "We did it," she said under her breath as the house lights came back up and conversation in the auditorium began to resume. "We just won state! I can't believe it!"

In her seven years as the one-act play sponsor and director at Trinity Springs High School, Melissa's productions came within an eyelash of making it to state a couple of times.

She really thought they had a trip to state in the bag with *Arsenic and Old Lace* a few years earlier, but it didn't make it out of the Regional contest, the last hurdle to advance to state. *You Can't Take it with You* also made it to Regionals but came up snake eyes.

Then again, she didn't have Katy Christoval in her cast either of those years. And as she watched Katy absolutely nail the shit out of playing Eliza Doolittle once again, she was mentally kicking herself for not recruiting Katy to try out for one-act play her freshman and sophomore years.

Melissa had always prided herself on finding students walking the halls she thought that, with a little encouragement, would do extremely well on the stage given a chance. She thought about how great Katy would have been as one of the aunts in *Arsenic and Old Lace*.

She remembered Katy initially coming in for her tryout. She was very pretty, and she didn't seem the least bit phased by trying her hand at acting for the very first time in her life.

Her stage presence was undeniable. Her demeanor in the spotlight was completely natural. Plus, Katy delivered each and every line with the conviction and confidence of a seasoned thespian. She *was* Eliza Doolittle when she was on that stage. She could even mostly disguise her Texas drawl.

"Are you positive you've never done this before?" Melissa asked her from the center of the little theater at Trinity Springs High School. Looking up into the lights shining down on her with a squint, Katy, who was literally standing on stage for the first time, replied, "No, ma'am."

Melissa made her way backstage, stopwatch in hand, as her cast continued to break down the set. They still had plenty of time to clear the stage since the actual production ran right on schedule.

She first made eye contact with Brady Burke, who played Professor Henry Higgins, as he carried a table off stage. Brady gave her a huge smile, which she reciprocated and gave him a thumbs-up while she nodded her approval.

Brady had been in one-act play since his freshman year. Melissa knew there probably wasn't anybody among her kids who would be more excited if they did indeed win the whole thing.

Brady, who had an affinity for Stanley Kubrick movies, had always loved acting, and the chemistry he and Katy shared on the stage was undeniable. Although everybody in the cast always did a great job, it was that chemistry between the two lead roles that was at the heart of *Pygmalion*'s success.

Hell, Melissa was not only expecting to win state, she figured Brady and Katy were shoo-ins to win Best Actor and Best Actress after their amazing performances.

As Melissa stood on the side of the stage and watched, she spotted Katy hurriedly carrying a lamp. Katy didn't see her right away, but when she finally did, she also smiled bigger than Melissa had ever seen her smile before, which was saying something.

"You were awesome!" Melissa mouthed to her. Katy mouthed, "Thanks," and scurried off stage to put down the lamp so she could get back and grab another prop to help finish clearing the set.

With five minutes still left of their allotted time and the stage almost completely clear, Melissa stepped outside to a hallway in the side of the theater to finally get a moment to herself on what had been an insanely busy day.

She and her kids had loaded up on the bus for Austin from the Trinity Springs parking lot at 6:30 a.m. The competition started at 10 a.m.

Of course, even though they were competing at state, there was no way Trinity Springs High School was going to foot the bill for hotel rooms in Austin, seeing as it was only 90 miles away. But that wasn't necessarily a bad thing.

Melissa thought about how much chaos it would be trying to keep tabs on a bunch of high school students staying in a hotel room the night before a big competition. She figured her kids would be much better off sleeping in their own beds and getting started early in the day.

The school did at least pony up for Shipley Do-Nuts and orange juice and milk for everybody for the drive to Austin. Melissa was nervous because she knew traffic would not be good at 8 a.m., so she wanted to make sure they got an early start.

They were a little more than halfway to Austin when Katy got up and walked to the front of the bus, where Melissa was seated directly behind the driver. The loud wave of conversation on the bus had finally started to calm down some by then, so Katy decided she would talk to Ms. Henderson for some advice.

"Do you have a couple of minutes, Ms. Henderson?"

"Of course, Katy. Sit down, sweetie, sit down."

Melissa, who was going over the rules and itinerary for the competition one last time, pretty much called everybody "sweetie." Katy slid into the seat next to her.

Katy took another sip of orange juice from the carton in her hand. She still had a little bit of glaze on the right side of her mouth from the doughnut she had just finished.

"I know this is the first time Trinity Springs has ever been to state in OAP. And I guess I'm just feeling a little, you know, nervous. I mean, there are going to be a lot of people there. More than we have every performed in front of, right?"

"You're right, Katy. This will be the biggest audience we've done the play for yet, but that's the *only* difference. It's going to be just like every other time we have done the play — at Zone, District, Area and Regionals.

"You know exactly what you're doing and all of your lines like the back of your hand. All you have to do is go out there and do it exactly the way you have been doing it this whole time.

"Katy, you are *so* talented. You have a very natural gift for acting. Every word that comes out of your mouth — out of Eliza's mouth — rings true. Believe me you were absolutely born to be on that stage."

"Oh, Ms. Henderson, thank you very much. That's so sweet. I do love acting. I never would have expected to love it nearly as much as I do.

"There's something really cool about becoming somebody else for a little while, you know? It kind of helps you see thing from a different perspective. Still, I think I'm going to be pretty nervous up there today."

"Katy, I want to tell you something I have never told any other student at Trinity Springs." Melissa paused and took a deep breath before continuing. "When I was in high school, I was in one-act play, too. And I loved it so much. I started my freshman year and did OAP every year."

"That's awesome, Ms. Henderson!"

"It really was awesome, Katy. I had a blast. And acting all throughout high school helped me decide to major in theater in college. I thought acting for a living would be fun, but I also imagined it would be really, really tough.

"Plus, I had no desire to move to California. I'm a Texas girl, through and through — just like you. Almost from the beginning of college, I knew I wanted to do exactly what I'm doing today — teach acting in high school and direct one-act plays. I know in my heart I made the right choice."

"I think we can all tell how much you love what you do, Ms. Henderson. You have such a passion for it. It's like you can see how everything about a play should look, sound and feel right from the beginning."

"I appreciate that very much, sweetie. But, what I really wanted to tell you about was that our one-act play my junior year went to state."

"Seriously? Oh, my God — just like us!"

"Exactly like us," Melissa said, looking out the window for a moment as the bus was rolling past Aquarena Springs in San Marcos.

"We did *Noises Off*. I played Brooke Ashton. It was one of those things where the cast had such tremendous chemistry — just like ours. Everybody loved everybody off stage, so that really came through when we performed. It was authentic. Authenticity is the key to great acting, Katy. You absolutely must be believable enough to convince the audience you are that character."

Katy nodded as she focused on every word Ms. Henderson was saying. Her Texas accent wasn't quite as thick as Katy's, but it was also undeniable.

"More than anything, Katy, to this day it's an experience that I count among the absolute best in my life. I still keep in touch with three or four of my fellow cast members from that year.

"The point is I can tell you that performing on that stage at state is no different than it was at any of our other competitions. Just picture yourself doing the play on our stage in the little theater. See it happening in your mind. You're going to do just fine."

Katy smiled again and felt reassured she could handle the pressure. Seeing how disappointed Graham was to get so close to state in basketball and not getting there was still fresh on her mind, providing her with a little bit of extra motivation.

She wished Graham and Erin could have come to watch her at state, but Katy also believed them not being there might help her be a little bit less nervous. And the pep talk helped immensely.

"Thanks so much, Ms. Henderson. I feel a lot better now."

"You're very welcome, Katy."

Katy got back up and walked back to the seat she was sitting it, right in front of Benjamin Sanger.

Melissa looked out the bus window again as the bus continued to barrel up I-35 toward the University of Texas. Her smile faded as she thought about *Noises Off*.

She hadn't told Katy the entire story about her experience acting in the play that year. Melissa had done an amazing job the first few competitions but totally tanked when they got to state.

She knew from her first line that she was just not on top of her game that morning as they were the first play to perform. She flubbed a couple of lines, which got her flustered and stuttering. She just felt uncomfortable and nervous the whole time. She almost knocked one of the props off a table.

There was never a doubt in her mind that she had cost them a shot at winning state. And it absolutely destroyed her. The play did not even finish in the top four.

Melissa cried on a regular basis for two weeks after state that year, and she spent her life trying to atone for not being at her best during her biggest moment in the spotlight. To make matters worse, their play didn't even make it past Area her senior year.

But when Katy Christoval walked into the Trinity Springs theater for tryouts, Melissa knew this could be the year she could finally scratch that insanely annoying itch.

She thanked God each and every night since Katy became that missing piece of the cast she was so desperately trying to fill. In fact, prior to Katy's audition, Melissa had no earthly idea who was going to play Eliza.

Now that she was going back to state as a participant for the first time since high school, it was almost too much for her brain to handle. She was determined to hold her shit together — this time as a director.

Melissa closed her eyes and wondered what it would be like to walk up to the front of that auditorium and have that state championship trophy in her hands as the bus barreled toward Austin. She smiled again as she saw it happen, just like Vernon saw himself winning state at the Frank Erwin Center right down the road.

Melissa finally snapped back into the present as she made her way backstage to see the kids after their flawless performance. She couldn't stop smiling.

When she got backstage, there was an eruption of joy like they had already won state. Melissa smiled and told everybody not to count their chickens before they hatch, to get dressed and help load the set on the bus before the awards ceremony, which was still about an hour or so away.

"We've got some snacks on the bus if you need anything. And we'll stop and eat on the way back."

"Can we go to Mr. Gatti's for pizza?" Brady asked emphatically.

"Brady, if we win state, we can go any damn place you want, sweetie!"

Melissa spent the next nervous minutes walking around outside and trying to contain her excitement while her kids prepared for the awards ceremony. The crisp air outside only added to her adrenaline.

"We did it," she said out loud as she strolled around the University of Texas campus near the auditorium and watched other directors, students and parents mill about and get some fresh air, too. "I just know we did."

Melissa eventually made her way back inside the theater with 10 minutes to spare. When she walked back into the auditorium, most of her cast was already sitting comfortably, stage right, in the first three rows. It was their lucky spot. They had sat in that exact spot in each auditorium after each competition.

They all looked up and smiled at her as she sat down on the end of the front row. As Melissa settled in and looked around, she noticed Katy wasn't there. After two or three more minutes passed, she turned to the row behind her and asked if anybody knew where Katy had gone.

"She's talking to some dude outside. I think it's somebody she used to go to school with when she lived here or something. I don't think she knew he was going to be here," Brady said.

Melissa didn't want anybody — especially Katy — to miss the awards ceremony. "I'm going to get her," Melissa said, her ass already having left the seat.

She scurried up the aisle and out the main theater doors. She stopped and looked around, when she spotted Katy talking to some kid who looked like Ren McCormack from *Footloose*. Melissa walked up to them, getting their attention when she got closer.

"Katy, we've got to get back in there right now. The awards ceremony starts in just a few minutes."

"Okay, Ms. Henderson. This is Tyler. We used to go to elementary school together and roller skating at Rollin' 'Cross Texas on the weekends when I lived here. I haven't seen him since right after I moved to Trinity Springs in fifth grade. Can you believe that? He's doing sound for his school's play."

"Nice to meet you, Tyler. Let's go, Katy! The awards ceremony is about to start."

"Yes, ma'am. Goodbye, Tyler. It was really great seeing you again. Good luck."

"Good luck to you, too, Katy," Tyler said with a grin, giving Katy a quick hug.

Melissa grabbed Katy's hand as they made their way back into the auditorium just as the judges were making their way back in to deliver the results to the anxious waiting crowd.

First were the individual awards. After the honorable mentions and All-Star Cast announcements, the judge who was announcing the results said, "Best Actress goes to ... Katy Christoval, Trinity Springs."

Her cast mates erupted in yells and screams as Katy, looking completely dazed, got up to accept her medal. She walked right in front of Tyler Nixon, who made eye contact with her and gave her a couple of golf claps. Katy smiled from ear to ear back at him.

The entire auditorium continued to clap loudly as she started back to her seat. After the announcements for Best Actor, which Brady won, and Best Director, which Melissa did not win, the judge started to announce the runner-up plays. Third runner-up, second-runner up and first runner-up — and Trinity Springs wasn't among the three of them, which meant, of course ...

"And your 1986 Class 3A One-Act Play state champions ... *Pygmalion*, Trinity Springs High School."

The whole Trinity Springs cast erupted yet again, some of them jumping up and down and screaming. Katy put her hands over her mouth and started to cry tears of joy.

Melissa walked up to get their trophy and felt like she might faint as her knees felt like butter. This time, however, she absolutely nailed it. She got the award and immediately raised the trophy high above her head in celebration while looking at her group.

None of what was happening seemed real to her at all. And the giant weight that had been on her shoulders since high school was finally mercifully lifted.

Not caring in the least she did not win Best Director, Melissa practically ran back to her cast and held the trophy up again as they all jumped up and down and touched the trophy.

"Thank you all for coming," one of the other judges said, having to raise his voice over the Trinity Springs contingent. "We hope to see you all again next year. Let's give all of our schools another round of applause."

The celebration continued as Melissa made her way around the group and gave each of them a hug with the thunderous applause of the crowd as background noise. She finally got to Katy, who was grinning with her Best Actress medal dangling from her neck.

"Oh my God, Ms. Henderson. We did it! We really did it!"

"We sure did, Katy. And you got Best Actress, too. I'm so happy for you —for us."

"I am, too. I think this might just be the best day of my life."

A couple of seconds later, Tyler walked up to Katy and gave her another hug.

"Congrats, Katy C. Great job. It was so good to see you. We need to make sure it doesn't take so long to see each other again."

10

VICTORIA CHRISTOVAL

Graham woke up before his alarm went off on Thursday morning.

He didn't even bother to look at the time as he reached over and silenced the alarm before as he stumbled out of bed.

Graham walked into the kitchen, poured himself a bowl of Count Chocula and plopped down at the kitchen table.

He realized as he started to eat breakfast he had not read one damn word of *Wuthering Heights* the night before, which meant he still had three lovely chapters to look forward to reading when he got home from school.

Ah, Christ. More damn Wuthering Heights tonight. Great.

Had he not known about the pop quiz coming up on Friday, he probably would have just blown the assignment off all together. But he sure didn't want to start a new school year off with a big, fat "F" on his first English IV assignment. He was going to need all the help he could get in Vertigo's class.

It wasn't like he could have concentrated on reading anything the night before anyway. Even after Vernon's reassurances, Graham couldn't concentrate on anything other than thinking about seeing Katy again for the rest of the night.

He tossed and turned in bed, wondering what was going to happen with Tyler the next day at school, which led to Graham getting about three full hours of sleep.

"Good morning, honey," Donna said as she strolled into the kitchen in her robe. "You're up early for a Saturday."

Graham immediately stopped chewing and dropped his spoon into his bowl of cereal, causing a splatter of milk to fly onto the table.

He immediately knew "it" was happening — right fucking then, right fucking there. Graham was right. Tyler wasn't bullshitting. Not at all. Not one god damn bit, as a matter of fact.

Graham was going to see Katy again. And he knew the instant his mom said "Saturday" it was the day she died.

"Um, Saturday?" he managed to answer, as milk dribbled down from his mouth to his chin.

"Yes, dear," Donna said. "Saturday. Did you get up so early that it made you forget what day of the week it is?"

Graham started to feel a panicky feeling come over him again as he fumbled around for the newspaper on the kitchen table. He finally got hold of it and looked at the date on the front page. Sure enough, May 24, 1986.

"Holy fucking shit," Graham said under his breath. "Holy fucking shit. I can't believe this."

"Can't believe what, honey?"

"Nothing, Mom," he said, quickly picking up his bowl, which was still almost full, and dropping it into the sink so he could get out of the house as quickly as possible. "I didn't say anything at all."

Graham practically ran back to his room to see what time it was. 8:35 a.m.

Holy fucking shit. This is really happening.

He quickly got to the bathroom, undressed and hopped into the shower, turning on the water at the same time. The cold water jolted him, but he didn't relent. If he hurried, he might be able to catch Katy before she even left for Austin.

As he took the fastest shower of his life, clocking in a little less than a minute, Graham tried to remember all of the specifics of that day. It wasn't that hard, seeing as how he had gone over the details of that day over and over again the last three months.

For some reason, he kept picturing Katy in the convenience store getting herself a Dr Pepper and a pack of grape Bubble Yum for the road.

Should I try to catch her at E-Z Mart? What if I miss her at home while I'm doing that? Shit.

In disbelief that he was actually going to get to see Katy again, he remembered how he couldn't go with her to Austin that day because his Dad was coming into town to hang out with him and take him to dinner before he headed back to Big D.

Graham knew immediately that he'd have to try to keep that from happening before he could even think about trying to catch Katy.

He only saw his Dad about once every three or four months and during the holidays. Graham really looked forward to their time together, but he quickly had to think of an excuse to postpone. And hope to God his Dad hadn't left yet.

He remembered his Dad had showed up around 2 p.m. on that day. They had mostly hung out in town and talked about the Rangers and their 2-1 loss to Boston the night before.

Graham had given a little bit of thought to what he would do if Tyler wasn't kidding and it did end up being the day Katy died he got to see her again.

He was really glad he woke up early and had most of the day to locate her. Graham still wasn't sure exactly where to look if he had to track her down in Austin. Plus, he sure didn't expect the next fucking day after he told Tyler he wanted to go ahead and do it to be *the* day.

"Shit," Graham said as he rapidly dried off. "What the hell am I going to tell Dad? I have to catch Katy before she leaves for Austin. Shit, fuck, shit!"

Graham quickly got dressed and tried to calm down as he dialed his Dad's phone number. The finger he used to dial was shaking. The phone rang five times before he got a loud tone and that annoying message saying the number he dialed had been disconnected.

You've got to be fucking shitting me.

He slammed the phone down, picked it back up and dialed again, this time more carefully, figuring he had probably hurried and dialed wrong. This time, his Dad picked up the phone on the third ring.

"Hello," Miles said, surprised to hear his phone ringing so early on a Saturday. He had planned to leave around 9 a.m. to make the drive down to Trinity Springs.

"Dad," Graham said, almost yelling. "Dad, it's me. I have to cancel our day today. I'm sorry, but I just have something else really important I have to do that can't wait."

"Son, calm down. You sound upset. What is it you have to do?"

"I have to see Katy, Dad," Graham said, speaking in a little more of a normal tone as he tried his best to sound calm. "I know that doesn't sound like a big deal, but it is. Believe me, it really is."

Hearing the urgency in his son's voice, Miles assured his only child everything would be okay.

"We'll just push it back a week, son. Don't worry about it. Go see Katy, okay? I've got some errands I need to run today anyway. No big deal. I'll come down next Saturday instead. Will that work?"

"Yes. Thank you. Thank you so, so much. You have no idea how much that means to me. I love you, Dad."

"Okay, son. You two be careful."

Graham paused before replying, "We will."

He hung up the phone, relieved at how simple changing his plans with his Dad ended up being. Miles was a great guy, but he could be an absolute horse's ass sometimes when he didn't agree with something.

Graham figured cancelling on him would be a massive struggle. Now he just had to figure out a way to get the sudden change of plans past his Mom and get out of the house, ASAFP.

All the while, the fact that he was actually in the past — really, truly walking around and breathing in the past — kept popping into his mind as it raced in a million different directions.

I knew Tyler was telling me the truth. I knew it!

Graham knew he didn't have time to worry so much about time travel at the moment. When he looked in the mirror, he noticed his hair looked just a bit different than it had the day before, like he was almost due for a haircut.

That's just fucking freaky.

Graham gathered himself for a minute and walked into the hall, car keys in hand. He still needed to persuade his Mom he had a good reason for changing plans with his Dad. No matter what she said or how much resistance she put up, he was leaving that house in short order with the clock already ticking away.

Is it 24 hours from when I work up, or 24 hours from when it turned to midnight? Crap.

Graham briskly walked back into the kitchen, where Donna was eating her breakfast.

"Where are you going? I thought you and your Father had plans for today."

"We did. He had to back out on me."

"What?" Donna said, raising her voice. "That is not going to happen! He is not going to leave you high and dry at the last minute like that! You two had plans. I'm going to call him and give him a piece of —"

"Mom," Graham interrupted. "Mom, I'm sorry, I lied. It was me. I changed our plans. I just talked to Dad. He said it's cool. He said we could hang out next, um, Saturday."

"But why, honey?" Donna asked, her anger quickly turning to concern. "Why would you do that?"

"I have to see Katy today, Mom. I can't explain to you why, but I have to see her. It *has* to be today."

"Um, okay, sweetie. I thought she was going to Austin to go shopping today. Isn't that what you told me? And didn't you just see each other last night?"

"She is. And I did. I have to try to catch her. I'm sorry, Mom, I have to hurry up."

"Well, I'll come with you."

"No! It has to be just the two of us."

"What's going on here, Graham?"

"Mom, I'll explain it to you later. I swear to God I will. But right now I have to go! She's leaving any minute."

"When will you be back?" Donna asked as she watched Graham scurry out the front door, practically running.

"Late."

"How late?"

"I don't know, Mom, just late. I love you."

"Be careful," she said as he slammed the front door shut.

Whew!

Relieved to finally be in his driver's seat, Graham turned the key and backed out of the driveway. He was sure glad the good old *Trinity Springs Times* was there to confirm it was really three fucking months ago. Otherwise, he might still not be 100 percent convinced it was happening.

His mind raced as he indeed made a quick pass by the E-Z Mart to see if, by chance, he could catch Katy in that brief time she was there. No dice. The parking lot was empty with exception of the clerk's motorcycle.

Graham then made that familiar trip to Katy's house. As he drove, he looked around the inside of his car. It looked normal, but it was just a little bit different than it had the day before.

He reached over and grabbed a pile of his tapes. After shuffling through a few of them — *Purple Rain, Shout at the Devil* — Graham nearly ran off the road himself when he made his way to *The Unforgettable Fire*. His copy of that particular U2 tape had been destroyed when he accidentally ran over it in his driveway right after Kyle left for Colorado.

He didn't realize the tape had fallen out of his car until he heard the sound of it being crushed by his tires as he backed up. The gravity of the situation hit him square in the face as he looked at the tape that had been destroyed a couple of weeks ago reassembled and in perfect shape in his right hand.

He already believed it was May 24, but seeing that tape intensified the reality of the situation. He knew that he was about to see his dead girlfriend.

Holy shit. Holy fucking shit. This is crazy.

Graham was anxious to see if the 1979 white Ford Futura, Katy's mother's car, was in the driveway when he pulled up. Up until that very moment, that car would have been the last thing he would have ever wanted to see again.

As he rounded the corner onto Katy's street, he was practically shaking. Graham said a silent prayer that the car would be parked in the driveway, and that Katy was still home getting ready to leave for Austin.

But as he made out the shape of her house, he looked down and saw that the car, which had been parked in the driveway the night before, was gone.

That just fucking figures. Damn it!

Graham slammed on the brakes in front of Katy's house. He hurried to the front door and rang the bell.

He waited impatiently for what seemed like an eternity before Victoria Christoval finally opened the door, still in her pink bathrobe with a cup of steaming coffee in a #1 Mom mug in her right hand.

"Graham? What are you doing here, honey? It's so early."

"Mrs. Christoval, did Katy already leave for Austin?"

"Yes, about 20 minutes ago or so. She wanted to get an early start so she could get be there when the stores opened and get home before it gets dark. I thought you two talked about that last night."

Last night? Last night was in fucking September.

"Okay," Graham said, "Do you know where she was headed first?"

"Well, no, sweetie, I don't. Katy has lots of places she likes to shop in Austin. She'll probably go to Highland Mall and Northcross Mall. And probably some other stores here and there.

"I think she was looking for some summer clothes and some new shoes — maybe a new swimsuit so you two can take your annual trip to Schlitterbahn."

"Okay," Graham said, trying not to look too freaked out and appear normal while making mental notes of the places Victoria was rattling off. "I'm going to try to find her."

"Graham, honey, why don't you just wait until she gets home later today to see her? She said she would be back around 6:30. I can have her call you as soon as she gets back. We can all have dinner together. I'll make hamburgers."

"Thanks, anyway," Graham said as he quickly walked back to his car. "I appreciate it, Mrs. Christoval. I need to talk to her before then. I'm sure I'll find her. And I actually need to do some shopping myself anyway, so it works out perfectly."

Victoria watched Graham pull away before she finally closed the door. She looked at the back of the door for a few seconds, focusing on the peephole, while she thought about what had just happened.

Victoria hated lying to anybody — especially Graham. She had always really liked Graham, and she knew he treated her daughter very well. She knew he would not understand the real reason Katy had gone to Austin.

She let out a sigh, wondering what would happen if Graham happed to find Katy, but she figured there was almost zero chance of that happening.

As soon as Graham pulled his car to the end of Katy's street, he yelled as loud as he could. "Fuck! God damn it! If I had known for sure today was going to be the day, I would have been totally ready for it. Fuck you, Tyler Nixon, you son of a bitch!"

Once he got that out of his system, Graham knew he absolutely had to formulate a game plan. He had to be smart about this whole thing or he would never find Katy.

He knew he had to calmly look for her all around Austin. Every minute he wasted looking for her was one less minute he was going to be able to spend with her. He also had no idea what he was going to say to her to avoid sounding like he was absolutely looney tunes.

I can't be counter-productive. I have to be smart about this, or it will end up just being a wild goose chase. Stay calm, Graham.

Graham treated the task at hand like he did the last few minutes of a tight basketball game. He was almost always good at thinking things over before taking action. Cool as a cucumber under pressure.

As he struggled to drive the speed limit, Graham took out a small notebook and a pen from his small glove box. He jotted down the places Victoria had mentioned — Highland Mall, Northcross Mall.

He also wrote down a couple more spots where he knew Katy loved to shop — Waterloo Records, the Dobie Center Mall. Of course, she would drive by the state capitol at some point in the day. Maybe twice.

Graham thought about how he had to find Katy before she headed back home. And how, if he didn't, her mom's car would careen off FM 38 around 6:30 p.m., slam into a ditch, and flip over, killing Katy. Again.

He almost slipped into a daze as he drove along thinking about getting that phone call from Victoria telling him what had happened.

"Graham," Victoria said, her voice quivering. "Graham, my baby is dead. She died in a car accident. She was just a few miles from home, Graham. Oh, my God. She's gone. My Katy's gone."

Victoria then burst into hysterical crying. Graham did the same. The phone fell to the ground as Graham fell to his knees. For a few seconds after he heard the news about Katy, Graham literally could not see straight. He had to lie down on his bed and close his eyes as he was shaking.

That phone call still resonated in his mind liked it had happened yesterday. "I don't want to get that fucking phone call again. I'm not going to let it happen. I'm going to fucking stop this from happening."

Determined to save Katy, future circumstances be damned, he hit the accelerator and got on I-35 toward Austin a few minutes later.

"Not today."

11

KATY CHRISTOVAL

Graham pulled his Volkswagen into Austin right around 10:30 a.m. He had to sit through some traffic on I-35, of course, but it did at least give him some extra time to think about what he was going to say to Katy when he found her. If he found her.

He also thought about the fact he had to figure out a way to prevent her from getting into that damn accident if he couldn't find her. He still had no idea how he would try to convince her he had gone back in time. Graham was 99.9 percent sure Katy wouldn't believe him. He was worried she might freak out.

But, his mind was made up that he wasn't going to let this opportunity slip past him. He thought maybe he would just get her in his car and drive north until he was too tired to drive any more.

He figured maybe if he could get her as far away from the scene of the wreck at the time of the wreck, he would make sure it would never happen. If he did, he wondered if they would somehow be stuck in the past, which was just too overwhelming of a concept for him to put too much thought into.

When traffic came to a halt for a few minutes near Ben White Boulevard, he could so clearly imagine himself sitting next to Katy at their high school graduation in the Trinity Springs Auditorium, smiling with her whole life still in front of her.

Even in a cap and gown, in his imagination, she looked so incredibly beautiful. He thought about them maybe going to college together or even getting married someday, assuming he could stop her from dying.

After what seemed like an eternity, Graham finally found himself getting closer to downtown Austin. The urgency and adrenaline kicked in at the same time as he allowed himself to put more weight down on the accelerator.

He decided he would work his way up the city, so he took the 15th Street / MLK Boulevard exit to drive around the UT campus, and then to Waterloo Records.

Pretty much any time Katy went shopping, she brought something back for Graham. He looked down again at his U2 tape, which Katy bought for him after a shopping trip with her mom.

How is this happening?

He had little doubt it was going to take a whole lot of time and effort to track her down. He drove all around campus, all around the area near the state capitol and up and down 6th Street before making his way over to Waterloo, on Lamar.

Not surprisingly, there was no sign of Katy the first few places Graham looked. He figured it would have been entirely too much to ask for him to spot her that quickly.

Graham stopped in the Waterloo parking lot to collect his thoughts for a couple of minutes after he saw no sign of Victoria's car. He looked down at the clock on his dashboard again.

Where is she?

11:32 a.m.

Time to hit the malls.

First, he went to Highland Mall, which was just a couple of miles up I-35, north of downtown. He figured he'd be better off trying to spot her car rather than wandering around a mall trying to find her, seeing as how the clock was quickly starting to become his enemy.

Graham drove all around the parking lot, which was already fairly crowded, looking for that damn white Ford Futura. After two full sweeps, he was pretty certain Katy wasn't there. He was disappointed, but he knew damn well there was no time to dwell on it.

He figured he absolutely needed to find her no later than 4 p.m. so they'd have time to talk. She got in the wreck around 6:30, so she probably left Austin to come home around 4:45. Graham started to panic just a little bit when he checked the clock again.

11:45 a.m.

Jesus Christ. Come on, 'Slug Bug.' Don't fucking fail me now.

Next, Graham made his way across town to Northcross Mall. He got there right around noon.

As he was doing his sweep of that parking lot, his stomach started growling even louder than it did for cheese enchiladas on Monday. He remembered the bite or two of Count Chocula he had for breakfast.

That's just going to have to hold me for a while.

Graham started to get upset after not seeing Victoria's car at Northcross Mall. It was past noon. And for all he knew, Katy might have pulled into the Highland Mall parking lot five seconds after he pulled out.

"Fuck."

Graham decided that for the next hour or so he would just drive around Austin and then double back to the places he had already been. He knew finding her was starting to become like finding needle in a haystack.

One other idea finally came to mind. He dug in his car for some a couple of bucks worth of change, stopped at a phone booth and called Victoria. The phone rang about 12 times before he gave up and hung up.

He thought by some miracle she had heard from Katy, who had maybe told her more about her plans for the rest of the day.

As if she knew it was Graham calling, Victoria just let the phone ring. As it rang, she went into her daughter's room and grabbed a photo album out of Katy's closet with several pictures from when they used to live in Austin.

Victoria thought about all of the friends Katy had, and she felt bad again that Katy had to move her away from them in fifth grade.

She remembered how much fun Katy and her friends had buying baseball cards and roller skating. And, of course, they all adored Kiss. She completely understood why Katy wanted to see Tyler again and catch up more after she ran into him at state one-act play.

"You'll never believe who I saw," Katy told her a couple of hours after she got home from Austin after state. "Tyler. It was so cool to see him again."

Just as Graham hung up the phone, a familiar car passed him. It wasn't Victoria's Ford Futura, though. Instead, it was Coach Elgin's blue Dodge Ram pickup truck.

Graham thought for sure he had to be hallucinating from hunger. What were the fucking odds that Coach Hard-Ass was hanging out in Austin the day Katy died? He had never told Graham about being there that day.

Maybe he wasn't here the first time. God, this is so fucking weird.

When the truck stopped at a light, across the road, Graham looked over and noticed Coach Elgin had a woman in the truck with him that was clearly not Mrs. Coach Elgin. He could only make out her hair color, but Graham could have sworn the lady in the truck with him looked like Vertigo.

Coach Elgin's wife always brought cookies or brownies for the team for a postgame snack when they played home games on Friday nights. She was always super nice to Graham and all of his teammates. Plus, she was really hot, which didn't hurt a bit.

As the light turned green and Coach Elgin's truck pulled away, Graham's hunger pangs were approaching unbearable.

Damn it, I have to eat something. I can't find Katy if I pass out from hunger.

He decided he would have to hit the Whataburger drive-thru to get a combo meal to eat while he drove around. Double meat Whataburger with double cheese, Whata-sized with a Coke, naturally.

As he drove and looked for Katy, Graham ate his burger and fries and drank his Coke. It was almost 1:45 p.m. Graham still had no more idea where she was than when he got to town.

He had been back to Highland Mall, back to Waterloo, and then back to Northcross Mall with no luck at all. He had driven all over the UT campus and around the state capitol again.

About 45 minutes after he finished eating, he had to also stop to get some gas as the precious minutes continued to melt away.

While pumping his gas, Graham thought back to one day after school when he and Katy hung out after G-Hall and one-act play practice. They were home alone at Graham's house, in his room, sitting on his bed.

After making out for a few minutes, they started to talk about their upcoming senior year of high school.

"What's going to happen to us when we get to college, Graham?" she said. "Are we going to go to the same school? It's something we have to figure out soon, sweetie. I think I might want to go to UT."

The clicking of the gas pump shutting off brought Graham back to reality as those words rang in his ears.

"Where in the fuck is she?" he said under his breath as he closed his gas cap and jumped back in his car.

2:15 p.m.

Eventually, his heartbreak at not being able to find her turned back into anger at Tyler Nixon. Seriously, why the hell hadn't he warned Graham that he was going back to May 24 the next damn day? And if he wasn't going to get to see Katy, then what was the point? To torture him?

Just a little bit of a heads up would have allowed Graham to get up extra early and get over to Katy's house before she even left. Perhaps he could have stopped her from even going to Austin in the first place.

Graham figured that was precisely why Tyler hadn't told him it would be the next day — he had to somehow make things more difficult.

"That's such bullshit. I can't believe that son of a bitch would ..."

Suddenly, Graham had an idea. You could practically see the light bulb pop up over his head. With time running out, he knew he had to make something happen, do something totally different than he had been doing all day.

With a small smudge of ketchup on the lower right corner of his mouth, Graham got back out of his car and ran over to the phone book dangling from the payphone on the side of the gas station.

Graham hurriedly made his way to the white pages of the Austin phone book.

There were nine Nixons listed, but he remembered Tyler mentioning to him that he had lived in North Austin. There were only two Nixons listed in that part of town, one on North Lamar and one on Payton Gin. Graham was pretty sure the two addresses were located fairly close to each other, too.

At last, Graham caught his first real break of the day. He was already in North Austin. He couldn't believe it had taken him so long to think about looking up Tyler, although he wasn't sure what the hell he was going to say to him if they saw each other, either. After all, they hadn't technically even met at that point in time.

Hey, man, you don't know me, but you sent me back in time to find my dead girlfriend, so I could see her one last time and say goodbye. I was wondering if you, um, you might know where I can find her before she goes back home and dies again?

Shit, Tyler might threaten to kick my ass if I tell him that.

As he made his way over to Payton Gin a few minutes later, Graham looked at the page of the phone book with the two Nixons in north Austin listed on it he had torn out. He was getting close to the first address — home of Alvin and Winona Nixon. He glanced down at the clock.

2:55 p.m.

Alvin had better be getting fired from his job really damn soon!

Graham could feel the pressure start to mount as he thought again about how insane it was that he was driving around Austin three months prior to the present.

And even though Tyler had made it happen, just like he said he would, Graham was getting angrier and angrier by the minute thinking about how he was just about to piss away the whole day and his opportunity to see Katy again. For some reason, *Wuthering Heights* popped into his brain.

I must be delirious. Eighteen-fucking-oh-one.

He quickly forgot about the book he was dreading reading and thought about what he would do if he wasn't able to find Tyler at either of the two addresses.

Graham figured he would try to find Katy driving back to Trinity Springs before she got in the wreck, maybe even resorting to waving her down on the side of the road a few miles up FM 38.

That was Plan C. It was shitty, but it was all he had left if this didn't work. Then again, it might backfire. And then he'd have to actually see the wreck happen, which would be about the worst outcome he could possibly imagine.

His mind was racing, but it was nothing compared to what his mind did when he came up on the Nixon residence on Payton Gin, one block from North Lamar, and saw Victoria's Ford Futura, in all of its glory, sitting in front of the house.

What the hell?

Graham was so shocked, he ran up on the curb slamming on the brakes as his brain tried to process what it was seeing. He couldn't get out of his car quickly enough. He left his door wide open and the engine running as he ran to the front door and started pounding it with his fists.

"Katy!" he bellowed. "Katy Christoval, get the hell out of there right now! What are you doing here? Nixon? Are you in there? Both of you — get out here right damn now!"

Graham noticed the curtain in the living room window moving. He kicked the door a couple of times, leaving footprints on the blue paint, before it finally opened up. Standing there in a black T-shirt and a pair of shorts and looking stunned and disheveled was Tyler Nixon.

The two of them just stared at each other for a few seconds. Then, Graham saw Katy emerge from behind Tyler. As pissed off as he was, his heart just sank at the sight of her.

She was wearing the outfit she had on when she died. And actually seeing her living and breathing in those clothes again, along with the fact she was with Tyler, made Graham's knees start to feel wobbly.

Of course she's wearing that. Today is the day she died.

"Graham," she yelled, trying to push past Tyler. "Graham, I can explain, sweetie."

But the turn of events was too much. Graham walked back to his car quickly and got in, with Katy repeatedly yelling his name and trailing him.

"Graham! Graham! I'm sorry, Graham. I made a mistake. Graham! Talk to me! Please don't go, Graham!"

Graham's head was about to explode. He got in the car and took one last look back at the two of them, standing there in the front yard with shell-shocked looks on their faces.

What the hell just happened? Katy and Tyler? Did I really just see that?

He slammed on the accelerator and headed toward North Lamar. Graham stopped for about a half second at the stop sign on the corner. He then buried his foot into the accelerator again without looking either way.

When he did, a massive Crete semi truck going about 50 miles per hour slammed into the side of his car. Not wearing his seat belt, Graham flew through the windshield and onto North Lamar as cars slammed on their brakes to avoid hitting his limp body in the road.

Katy and Tyler heard the horrible accident but were too far away to see exactly what had happened. They both ran the block up to North Lamar. And when Katy saw Graham lying in the street, she screamed, hurried over to him and knelt down, sobbing wildly in front of a crowd that had started to gather.

A couple of people also screamed at the sight of Graham, who was covered in glass and blood.

"Graham!" she screamed. "Graham, oh my God, what have I done to you, sweetie? Graham!"

Graham was dead on impact. Katy laid her head down on his chest and sobbed. She had never been filled with so much regret in her life. Katy had just driven 90 miles from home to cheat on her boyfriend, who had always loved her with all of his heart.

Tyler surveyed the whole scene in total disbelief. The driver of the truck had gone to call 9-1-1. A few minutes later, the sirens approaching in the distance mixed with the sound of Katy sobbing as dark clouds formed overhead.

Katy continued to grasp Graham's lifeless body, holding on tightly as paramedics and police officers arrived. They quickly cleared her out of the way.

"What have we done?" Tyler said, now standing a few feet away, on the side of the road near Katy. Much louder this time, he said. "What the hell have we done, Katy?" That caused her to finally look up and snap out of a daze.

She walked over to the curb and sat down in the rain that had started to fall. She stared out at the scene as her head throbbed and the paramedics were huddled over Graham. Her Hard Rock Café T-shirt was covered in blood from holding her dead boyfriend.

"Graham's dead," she muttered. "Oh, my God. He's dead. Oh, my God, Tyler."

Tyler looked directly into the rain, which was falling harder, looked back toward the scene of the accident as paramedics were covering up Graham's body, and then back at Katy again.

"Katy, who's Graham?"

12

KERMIT HENDERSON

After watching several of his friends graduate from Trinity Springs High School on Friday night, Kermit Henderson was wrapping up a pretty standard Saturday afternoon by burying jump shots in a pickup game on the outdoor courts at Ryan Park.

He was especially on fire since it was essentially the first day of summer vacation, which seemed to give him plenty of extra pep in his step and accuracy to his shots.

Kermit planned to do a lot of practicing over the summer after coming so close to state earlier in the year, but he was also excited about a family trip to New Orleans coming up.

Even though his family was planning to drive, which would be a crazy long car trip, Kermit had never been to the Big Easy before.

In fact, he was thinking about what it would be like to walk down Bourbon Street as he yelled "good" and drained the last shot of the day from 25 feet, rattling the chain link net.

The sun was starting to set, so he knew he had to get back home for dinner — especially since it was pizza night. He knew too well if he wasn't there by the time the pizza arrived, he'd be S.O.L.

"Nice shot, baby," Vernon Wiley said, running over to Kermit and giving him a sweaty celebratory hug. "That's what I'm talking about."

After chugging the last of their water, the two of them started walking back to their cars.

"We're almost seniors, dude," Vernon said. "Can you believe that shit? Seniors!"

"In 365 days, we're going to be out of this bitch. And you're going to be kicking it in El Paso."

"Um, 364," Vernon said, causing them both to laugh loudly.

"Alright then," Kermit said, reaching his hand out for Vernon to shake.

"I've got run to the store real quick for mom. Same time next week?"

"Bet. Same time next week," Vernon said, sliding into the driver's seat of his car. Kermit did the same. The two of them took off in opposite directions.

Kermit turned on his radio, which was playing Phil Collins' "Sussudio." He couldn't help but bounce his head a little bit as he headed home.

Man, I'm going to put a damn hurting on that pizza tonight, he said to himself. And then I am going to sleep my ass off for the next three months. I ain't waking up in no damn a.m. unless absolutely necessary.

As he caught a glimpse of himself in the rearview mirror, he mugged like he was getting ready to take his senior picture for the yearbook.

Just before Kermit made the turn onto FM 38, his car started to sputter. "Oh, no. What the fuck?" he asked as he looked down and saw the needle on his gas tank buried on "E."

"God damn it, I can't be out of gas on pizza night! Man, I don't believe this."

Of course, there was no traffic, so he pulled his car over to the side of the road. It was getting close to 6:30 p.m., which was when he was supposed to be home for dinner. The good news was he was only about a mile-and-a-half away, so he figured he could walk it and only be a little bit late.

Kermit's car was in a good spot, well off the road and away from any other cars that might come along.

He wiped the sweat off with his towel, which he decided he would take with him on his unplanned hike. He wished he had some water left, but figured he would walk pretty quickly and could drink all the water he needed when he got back to the house.

About a mile from Kermit on FM 38, Katy had her foot buried on the accelerator of her mother's car.

She had cried nonstop from Austin all the way back to Trinity Springs after she and Tyler had spoken to the police. Katy called her mother to tell her what had happened. Victoria was understandably devastated.

"Stay where you are, Katy," she said, sobbing. "We'll come get you."

"No, Mom. I want to get back home as soon as possible. I don't want to be here anymore. And we would still have to get my car back home. I'm leaving Tyler's house right now."

"Katy," Victoria said. "You're upset. Please, please be extra careful."

"I will."

The police told Katy they would call Donna and Miles to tell them what had happened to their son. Katy had to tell Tyler that Graham was her boyfriend she had not mentioned, even after Tyler had asked her if she had one.

Still covered in dried blood, she didn't know how she was going to face anybody in Trinity Springs after what had just happened. Katy felt sick in the pit of her stomach.

"What the hell were you thinking, Katy? This is all your fault. You're so stupid."

She sat in silence as her car reached almost 80 mph on the last stretch home. She started to cry again, so she reached onto her passenger seat for the open package of Kleenex next to an empty bottle of Dr Pepper.

Katy wondered why Graham had gone to Austin in the first place. And how on earth had he possibly found her at Tyler's house?

A MATTER OF LIFE AND DEATH IN TEXAS

When she looked back up, she saw Kermit walking very close to the road and in even closer proximity to her.

"Holy shit," she screamed as she slammed on the brakes to avoid hitting him. Kermit understandably almost shit his pants as he watched Victoria's car loudly squeal right in front of him in the blink of an eye. He was completely frozen in fear as Katy was frantically turning the wheel to her right.

She somehow narrowly avoided plowing into him, but the car slid into the side of the embankment, rolled over and flipped three times. It finally came to a rest up against a barbed wire fence beyond the embankment on the side of the road.

"Oh, shit!" Kermit yelled, as he ran over to the car, which was upside down and still making all sorts of popping noises. Kermit dropped down to the ground and looked inside. He yelled again, "Oh my God, Katy! No!"

Kermit struggled to pull her out of the car, worried it would burst into flames, but when he finally did he could tell immediately she was dead. He sat down in the road and started to cry.

"What happened, Katy? How am I going to tell Graham?"

-30-

www.ingramcontent.com/pod-product-compliance
Lightning Source LLC
Chambersburg PA
CBHW061442040426
42450CB00007B/1167